Sigmund Brouwer

orca sports

Orca Book Publishers

Library and Archives Canada Cataloguing in Publication
Brouwer, Sigmund, 1959-

Tiger threat / Sigmund Brouwer.

(Orca sports)

ISBN 10: 1-55143-639-6
ISBN 13: 978-1-55143-639-5

I. Title. II. Series.
PS8553.R68467T53 2006 jC813'.54 C2006-903494-X
Summary: The Russian mafia is after Ray's roommate.

First published in the United States, 2006
Library of Congress Control Number: 2006929014

Orca Book Publishers gratefully acknowledges the support for its publishing programs provided by the following agencies: the Government of Canada through the Book Publishing Industry Development Program and the Canada Council for the Arts, and the Province of British Columbia through the BC Arts Council and the Book Publishing Tax Credit.

Cover design: Doug McCaffry
Cover photography: Fotosearch

Orca Book Publishers
PO Box 5626, Stn. B
Victoria, BC Canada
V8R 6S4

Orca Book Publishers
PO Box 468
Custer, WA USA
98240-0468

www.orcabook.com
Printed and bound in Canada.
Printed on 100% PCW recycled paper.

010 09 08 07 • 5 4 3 2

To Jordy Quinn

chapter one

Ever seen a little kid stick his finger in his nose and dig around for a bit? Just thinking about it makes you squirm. But have you ever noticed that you can't look away, even when the kid pulls something out and stares at it like he's going to eat it. Worse, when he decides he's actually going to eat it and starts putting his finger toward his open mouth, everything inside you silently screams to look away. You can't though. You have to watch until it's over, just like you can't look away from two cars about to hit at an intersection.

And ever had one of those dreams where you have to run to get away from something? A grizzly bear, maybe. A train coming down the tracks. Worse, a math teacher chasing you to give extra homework. It's the dream where you try to lift your feet, but powerful mud is sucking at them. No matter how hard you try to run, it feels like you are in a bubble where time has stopped. The danger outside your dream bubble heads toward you in terrible slow motion that lets you see every terrifying detail.

That's what it was like for me on a warm day in Medicine Hat, a couple of days after Christmas. I was standing beside my Jeep TJ, unable to turn my eyes from something about to happen in the backyard that was like two cars about to collide. Like being in a terrible dream, it seemed like I was in a bubble, too far away to stop what was about to happen to the Russian hockey player, but so close it seemed to unfold in slow motion.

I knew as I was watching who would get in trouble for it.

Me. Ray Hockaday. Center for the Medicine Hat Tigers in the Western Hockey League, trying to make the NHL.

The Russian also played for the Tigers. It was my job to protect him. But all I did was stand there with one of his teeth in my jacket pocket.

Worse, what unfolded in front of me was only the beginning of the trouble that followed.

The tooth was in a Ziploc bag in my jean-jacket pocket because three hours earlier I'd taken La-Dee-Dah to the dentist.

La-Dee-Dah was tall, skinny. Dark-haired. His face was all angles. Black eyes. Didn't speak any English. Not only one of the best sixteen-year-old left wingers in the WHL, but one of the best, period. Which is saying a lot, because he was competing against players as old as twenty. That, of course, was the reason he was in Canada, not Siberia or whatever part of Russia he grew up in.

His name, of course, wasn't really La-Dee-Dah, but Vladislav. Vladislav Malininich.

I had first met him two weeks earlier at my billet's house in Medicine Hat, a really big place on the South Saskatchewan River. Our coach had brought him over and told me that I was supposed to help Vladislav with just about everything, because this was the first time Vladislav had been out of Russia.

I had shaken his hand and had tried saying his first name.

Nyet, the kid had said in a voice that was surprisingly deep and slow for someone so skinny. *Me name vlah-dee-SLAHV.*

Later I would learn that *nyet* is "no" in Russian. I would also learn that he hated it when people mispronounced his name. He was constantly correcting them by saying it the way he wanted it said, emphasizing the end of his name: vlah-dee-SLAHV. That's when the guys started calling him La-Dee-DAH.

He got mad for a while, but after a couple of games, he realized we called him that because we liked him. That he was fitting in because we'd given him a special nickname that only guys on the team would use. And once he started laughing when we called him La-Dee-DAH, we also started calling him by his Russian nickname. Vlad.

See how it works with guys? Insults. They don't see another guy in the dressing room and tell him that it looks like he's losing weight or that he's got great hair or that the brown sweater is a good color for him because it brings out the brown in his eyes. That's how girls talk. No, when guys insult each other, it means we care. Girls need to figure that out.

I had taken Vlad to the dentist because he can't drive, has a terrible sense of direction, always gets bus routes mixed up and, when he's lost, can't speak English to ask for help.

And also because he has horrible teeth. Where Vlad grew up, dentists were the guys with pliers. Teeth didn't get fixed. Teeth got yanked.

The dentist was our team dentist. Dr. Dempster. Nice guy. Middle-aged. Marathon runner.

I had been sitting in the waiting room reading a *Sports Illustrated* when I heard loud screaming. *Nyet! Nyet! Nyet!*

Since that was about the only Russian word I knew, and I could guess who was saying it, it seemed like a good idea to find out what was happening. Especially when Dr. Dempster's assistant came running out for help.

I followed her back to the chair, where Vlad was pointing at the needle in Dr. Dempster's hand and still shouting *nyet*.

"Do you want me to translate?" I asked Dr. Dempster.

"I think I'm able to figure it out," Dr. Dempster said. "I'll give him ivy instead. He's lucky we're one of the few places in town set up to do that."

"Ivy?" I asked. "Like those creeping vines?"

"I. V." He smiled. "Intravenous drip. It will knock him out and he won't feel a thing.

Think Vlad can understand that?"

"You'll still have to put a needle in his arm, right?" I said.

"Right," Dr. Dempster said. "Any way you can convince him to let me do that? He needs a lot of work on those teeth."

I turned to Vlad. I pretended my forefinger was a needle and pushed it into my arm. Then I put my hands together, lifted them to my head, leaned my ear against my hands and closed my eyes as if I was sleeping. He understood but shook his head.

"Hey, La-Dee-Dah," I said. I then used two words that I had been teaching Vlad in English in the short time that I'd known him. "Trust me."

Finally, Vlad nodded slowly.

"Glad that's settled," Dr. Dempster said. "There's just one thing, Ray. Vlad might be a little loopy when he gets out of it."

"Loopy?"

"Loopy. It takes longer for some people to recover than others. So really watch him closely for a few hours after he gets out of the chair."

Watch him closely.

That's the part I didn't remember until it was too late.

chapter two

I had been billeting with the Moore family for two years. It was great. He was a banker and she was a kindergarten teacher. Their kids had grown up and left the house. So now they helped the Medicine Hat Tigers by giving players a place to stay during the season.

Not only were they nice, but they lived in a nice location. At night, with the window open, I heard the water of the South Saskatchewan River. Because they had large trees and there was a nature preserve close by, I could also hear owls at night and sometimes coyotes.

Often I'd wake up in the morning and look out my window to see deer or rabbits on the lawn in the shadows of the trees. Once in a while I'd even see a fox. It was like living in the country, except in the city. The only thing that ever disturbed the peace and quiet was the dog that belonged to the Moores.

This was Pookie, a nasty Chihuahua. You know what Chihuahuas are like. Tiny but always trying to make up for it by yapping. Pookie liked to bite too, with sharp little teeth that drew blood on my ankles. But somewhere in his peanut-sized brain he knew that someone big like me would be ashamed to actually fight back, so all I ever did after he nipped me was sigh and look for a bandage.

On that warm winter day, I pulled up to my parking spot behind the fence at the Moores' backyard. It was nearly twilight, and the breeze was gentle.

I was glad to finally reach the Moores' house. Since leaving the dentist, Vlad had been yodeling some crazy Russian tune. Seriously. He had even yodeled in the store where we stopped to buy milk and bread. He was yodeling as I shut the Jeep's motor off.

"Come on, La-dee-dah," I said. "Enough with the singing."

He gave me a loopy grin and yodeled more.

"Nyet," I said. "Don't you know what that means? Nyet."

More yodeling.

"Yeah," I said. I patted my jean-jacket pocket. It held a plastic Ziploc bag with one of Vlad's teeth, given to me by Dr. Dempster. "See if I give you your tooth. No money under your pillow for you tomorrow morning from the tooth fairy."

More yodeling.

It didn't seem like the time to try to explain the concept of the tooth fairy to him.

Vlad staggered through the gate into the backyard while I went to the back of the Jeep for the grocery bags. It was obvious the guy was still feeling good.

"Kitty! Kitty!" I heard him say in a happy voice. During the Christmas break, he'd been watching cartoons to learn English. "Kitty! Kitty!"

I looked up with a degree of hopefulness. A cat? In the Moores' yard? Pookie would be bolting out through the doggie door at any second to yap at me and Vlad. If I were lucky, the cat would be big enough to teach Pookie the lesson in manners that I wished I could.

I didn't see Pookie though.

Nor did I see a cat.

Instead I saw a skunk on the sidewalk at the Moores' back steps. It must have wandered in from the trees along the river.

"Kitty! Kitty!" Vlad said in the kind of voice that women use when they see babies. Vlad held his arms out to the skunk, weaving a little from side to side. "Kitty! Kitty!"

Only then did I remember Dr. Dempster's advice. *Vlad might be a little loopy...It takes longer for some people to recover than others. So really watch him closely for a few hours...*

"Nyet!" I shouted at Vlad. "Nyet!"

He must have thought I was still talking about his yodeling, because he took a few more steps toward the skunk.

The skunk stamped its feet. This, I remembered from the Nature channel, was a warning.

"Nyet!" I shouted again. "Nyet!"

I should have dropped the milk and the bread and jumped over the fence and tackled Vlad before he could reach the skunk. But I was frozen there, like in a bad dream. Unable to look away. Unable to move.

"Nyet!" I tried, even louder.

All this did was alert Pookie to the fact that we had arrived home and he could jump through the little doggie door and begin to terrorize our ankles.

I heard joyful yapping from inside the house. I could picture Pookie's little legs scrambling as he slid across the kitchen floor toward the back door.

Vlad had reached the skunk.

"Kitty! Kitty!" he crooned.

Vlad reached forward to scoop the skunk into his arms. He tipped a little and fell to his knees. At the same time, the skunk turned around and lifted its tail.

"Nyet!" I hollered.

Too late.

Vlad grabbed the skunk just as it let loose a full spray in Vlad's face, and just as Pookie made it through the doggie door at full speed and at full yap.

Vlad dropped the skunk. It landed on all fours and spun around to face the new danger, Pookie.

For a second, Pookie probably thought it was a cat too. But only for a second.

The skunk turned. It must have had plenty in reserve because, almost instantly, Pookie's yapping became high-pitched howls of terror. Pookie jumped back up the steps and back through the doggie door into the house. Seconds later I heard yelling from the kitchen that managed to drown out Pookie's howling.

Vlad was now rolling on the ground, clutching his face.

As the yelling got louder in the Moore house, the back door opened, throwing light into the yard.

Mr. Moore was still yelling about the awful smell in the house as he pitched Pookie down the steps. Pookie landed on Vlad. Vlad began to throw up. Pookie pawed at his little nose and a second later began to throw up on Vlad.

The skunk walked away with triumphant dignity, right down the sidewalk toward me. I jumped back to my Jeep and stood on the hood to give him plenty of room.

And through all of this, the horrible smell of skunk drifted through the air, making me gag where I waited on the hood of the Jeep for the skunk to leave.

chapter three

The first surprise when the season resumed four days later was that the Tigers had a new coach. Jim Dobbs, the coach who had started the season, had been offered a position in the NHL during the Christmas break. The Tigers had hired Blaine Thomas, who had been an assistant coach for one of the other WHL teams. The press conference to announce this was scheduled for the afternoon after our practice.

The second surprise happened twenty minutes into practice, when Blaine Thomas pulled me aside and told me I had five games to prove myself as a hockey player or I would be benched for the rest of the season.

I couldn't believe what I was hearing.

"Did you say benched?" I asked.

In the background I heard whistles as the other coaches worked some drills. There were the sounds of pucks slapping against sticks, of skates spraying ice. Some hollering. The guys on the rest of the team were continuing with practice, totally unaware that I'd just been blindsided.

"For the rest of the season," Coach Thomas said. "Unless I can trade you to another team."

He and I were standing near the bench. I was taller than him by at least five inches. He wore team sweats and a Tigers ball cap. He was barrel-chested, but not fat. Short red hair, lots of freckles. About my dad's age, maybe mid-forties.

"Benched," I repeated. I couldn't think of a thing I had done wrong. Especially since only twenty minutes had passed since he'd stepped onto the ice and introduced himself as head coach.

"Are you deaf too?"

I cocked my head. Sweat dripped from the inside of my helmet down my neck. "Too?"

"Well, I know for sure that you're afraid to go into the boards. By the way you repeat everything I say as a question, I've got to wonder if you're deaf too."

"I'm not deaf," I said.

"But you are afraid to go into the boards."

I looked away. Couldn't answer.

"I'm right here," Coach Thomas said. "Not somewhere in the stands."

I looked back at him.

"Afraid of me too?" he asked.

"You know how many goals and assists I have this season, right?"

"Of course I do," he said. "You're a tremendously skilled player."

"And you know my plus-minus is solid."

"Yup."

"But you're going to bench me," I said, "because you think I'm afraid to go into the boards."

"So look me in the eyes and tell me that you're not afraid."

My mouth was suddenly dry.

"This is your second year in the league," he said. "I think I've seen you play against my old team about twenty times. I can't remember one time you went into the boards first for a puck. The only penalties I ever saw you take were for tripping or hooking. Never elbowing, fighting. You don't mind using the stick against other players, but you're afraid to get in close."

I swallowed. It didn't help the dryness.

"Think the first set of drills today was an accident?" he asked.

I knew the drills he meant. Dump and chase.

"I wanted to see what you'd do. And I got my answer. Nothing. You're one of the fast guys on the ice, but the way you waited to go into the corner for the puck made sure even an overweight goalie would get there first."

"It's practice," I said. "I didn't want to..." I stopped, knowing how lame it sounded.

"You didn't want to get hurt."

I nodded.

"What's your dad going to say if you get cut and he learns why?" Coach Thomas asked.

Fear coiled in my stomach like a snake. My dad had played in the NHL twenty years earlier. He'd been known as an enforcer. One of the toughest guys in the league. He was just as tough at home.

"You need to understand something here, Ray," Coach Thomas said. "It's taken me fifteen years of a hundred percent effort to get to a head-coaching position in the WHL. I'm not going to lose it because players on this team won't put in a hundred percent themselves. The Tigers need to be tougher, and you can either lead the way. Or get out of the way. What's your decision?"

I was looking past him again. At the far side of the rink.

"Look at me," he snarled.

"But–"

"Look at me!"

I looked at him. "Coach, there's something wrong."

"That's why we're talking," he said.

"No," I said. "There's smoke."

"Smoke?"

This wasn't the time to ask him if he was deaf, like he'd asked me when I repeated things.

At the far side of the arena, billows of black smoke were coming out of the stands.

"Smoke," I said, wondering if it was my imagination.

It wasn't.

As Coach Thomas turned to look where I was pointing, fire alarms all through the arena began a clang that drowned out whatever he was about to say.

Coach Thomas blew his whistle. But none of the players heard him above the fire alarms.

And the mushroom of smoke grew bigger and blacker.

chapter four

"Tomato juice," I said. "The Moores made La-Dee-Dah soak in a bathtub full of tomato juice. But that wasn't the funniest part."

The entire team had been standing outside the arena for half an hour, waiting for the fire department to declare it safe to go inside. Coach Thomas had rushed all of us off the ice at the back and out through the doors that the Zamboni used to dump snow. We were still in our hockey gear and sweaters. One of the trainers had brought out tape for us to put along the bottom of our blades to protect them from the pavement.

"What could be funnier than La-Dee-Dah picking up a skunk because he thought it was a cat?"

This was from Todd Bailey, a gronk of a defenseman. He was one of five guys gathered in a circle around me as I told them about Vlad and the dentist and the skunk and Pookie.

"You have to picture it," I said. "La-Dee-Dah is on his knees choking from the skunk spray. Pookie's yelping inside the house, taking the skunk smell with him everywhere. Kitchen, living room. Pookie jumps into Mrs. Moore's lap, and now she's screaming because the skunk smell is on her. Mr. Moore pitches Pookie outside, Pookie lands on La-Dee-Dah and both of them are throwing up on each other."

I paused, knowing all of them were hanging on every word. They had no doubt the story was true. Vlad still faintly smelled of skunk.

"But it got worse," I said. "Much worse."

Another pause. I should have been enjoying this. There was a chinook wind in the Hat, so it was pleasant to be outside with my friends. Instead, half of my mind was on what Coach Thomas had asked me to decide.

Was I going to lead the way? Or be forced to get out of the way?

I was a good hockey player, close to great actually. So good that no one else had cared how tough I was. But no one else had figured out the truth.

Yes. I was afraid. I always played afraid. Afraid of injuries, afraid of pain. And, most of all, afraid that my dad would find out I was afraid.

"So what happened next?" one of the guys asked. "Pookie and La-Dee-Dah are throwing up on each other. Then what?"

"Mr. Moore stands in the doorway and starts yelling at La-Dee-Dah to tell him what happened."

"La-Dee-Dah can't speak English," Todd Bailey said.

"Exactly. You should have heard. Mr. Moore yelling at La-Dee-Dah in English.

La-Dee-Dah rolling on the ground and yelling at Mr. Moore in Russian. And Pookie yelping and pawing his face and throwing up all over again."

More laughter.

Vlad wandered over. He knew we were talking about him.

"Not kitty-kitty," Vlad said, grinning. He tried out two English words I'd taught him. "Stoo-pid skoonk."

We howled at that, and he joined in. Then Vlad lifted his right hand and squeezed it and made a whooshing sound.

"Exactly," I said. "Mr. Moore tells La-Dee-Dah to strip down to his undies. La-Dee-Dah doesn't understand a word. So I have to go up to him and try to explain. It's not working. So Mr. Moore starts yelling at me to do a better job. Like it's my fault that La-Dee-Dah can't speak English and my fault that La-Dee-Dah was so loopy after the dentist that he thought a skunk was a cat."

"Stoo-pid skoonk," Vlad said, nodding his head.

"So," I said, "all I can think of is to strip

down to my undies and point at La-Dee-Dah to do the same."

Again, Vlad lifted his right hand and squeezed it and made a whooshing sound.

"What's that?" Todd asked. All the guys were listening by now.

"The garden hose," I said. "As soon as La-Dee-Dah is down to his undies, Mr. Moore hoses him down with cold water for at least a half hour."

Vlad knew what I was talking about. He hugged himself with his arms and made a shivering motion. "Stoo-pid skoonk."

"Yes," I said. "Stoo-pid skoonk. I end up going to the grocery store to buy as many cases of tomato juice as they had. And the Moores burned Vlad's clothes."

"What about Pookie?" Todd asked. "They burn him too?"

"Very funny," I said, not meaning it. "Pookie still smells like skunk. He's been forced to sleep outside every night."

I shook my head. "It sure has messed up the little dog. Before, when he saw a cat, he'd chase it up a tree. Now he sees one, he starts whimpering and buries his nose under his paws. He must think all cats have a secret weapon like skunk spray."

More laughter.

And that's how the spirit of the team stayed. In a great mood. Especially when Coach Thomas came over and told us the firemen didn't know what had caused the fire. The rink was safe, but there was no sense trying to practice so we might as well get dressed and go home.

Except when we got back to the Tigers' dressing room, it smelled like skunk.

For good reason. Pookie was in the middle of the dressing room. Wrapped in hockey tape. Hanging from a skate lace tied to a light fixture.

chapter five

In the high school library that afternoon, I smiled at the beautiful girl who had spent the previous hour helping me with math. I closed the textbook.

"What a stupid I am," I said to her.

She giggled. "That's funny."

"Actually," I said, "there's a math story behind it. It's very sad. Just like my attempts at this homework."

"Really." She leaned forward at the table, resting her beautiful chin on her beautiful hands, giving me a beautiful smile. Her name was Amanda Kessler. She had long dark hair. She was wearing a light blue sweater that looked great with her long dark hair. Did I happen to mention she was beautiful? She was also the reason I pretended to be so stupid with math. So she would spend time with me to help me with it. "And what is that story, Ray?"

I was happy to tell her. It would take my mind off the questions about the horrible thing that had been done to Pookie in the locker room. The little dog hadn't been hurt, just very scared. It was enough to make me forgive it for all the times it had nipped my ankles.

What a stupid I am. If you're not brilliant –like me–the next best thing to do is use brilliant lines from stories or movies. Like when you're caught doing something and you're about to get in trouble, use the line from the scene in the animated movie called *Madagascar*, when police in Grand Central Station surround the two monkeys escaped from the zoo. Speak in a British accent and say this, just like one of the monkeys did: *If you have any poo, fling it now.* If this doesn't sound funny on paper, trust me, it was funny when the monkeys said it.

What a stupid I am. I learned about it in a sports book. See, once I wasn't good at reading, but I had a teacher who said that all reading helped you be a better reader. Just like practice in skating made you a better skater. He let me read sports stories, sports articles and sports books all year. He was right. After enough practice, I did become a better reader.

What a stupid I am.

I explained the story to Amanda.

It happened in 1968 at the famous Masters tournament in golf. A guy by the name of Roberto De Vicenzo–roll a name like that off your tongue and what girl wouldn't be impressed–had just tied the Masters to go into a playoff. Except he signed his scorecard without adding it up correctly. His playing partner had written down a four on a par three instead of the three that De Vicenzo had shot. But in golf, once you've signed your scorecard, you have to stick with it. If it's lower than you scored, you get disqualified. If it's higher than you scored, you have to stick with the higher score. So De Vicenzo had to keep the wrong score, which was one stroke higher. It put him out of the playoff. He was from Argentina and didn't speak English too well. That's when he said the line to reporters that made him famous. *What a stupid I am.*

"See," Amanda said when I finished my story, "math is important."

"Very, very important," I agreed. "So maybe we better meet tomorrow to work on my homework again?"

"And maybe you have some gum?"

I noticed she avoided my question, but I hid my disappointment. I did what any guy would do in that situation. I looked for gum.

I was wearing my jean jacket, so I patted the chest pockets.

There was something in the right front pocket.

I opened it. Felt the crinkling of a Ziploc plastic bag. Remembered what it was.

"Not that," I said.

"Not what?" she said.

"You really don't want to know," I said.

"I really do want to know," she said.

I pulled out the Ziploc bag. "It goes in your mouth, but it's not gum."

"Gross," she said. "A tooth."

It was Vlad's tooth. In all the confusion after he'd tried picking up a skunk, I'd forgotten to give it to him.

I shook the bag. "It's a Russian tooth."

She pointed and corrected me. "Actually, it's now a broken Russian tooth."

I looked closely. It *had* broken in two. Part of it was the roots of the tooth. The other part was a crown that had fallen off the tooth.

I looked even more closely. "That's weird."

"What?"

I opened the bag and shook out the pieces on the table. "Look. There's a tiny capsule too."

I picked up the pieces of the tooth and squinted. The crown and the bottom half easily fit together. I pulled them apart and looked into the center of the crown. There was a small indentation in the gold of the crown. In the inside of the crown.

"Do you have tweezers?" I asked. Not many–actually none–of the guys on the hockey team carried tweezers with them. Or eyeliner. Or lipstick. But Amanda was definitely not a guy. Or on the team. So I figured my chances were good.

Amanda nodded. She dug into her purse.

"Look at this," I said. I used the tweezers to pick up the small capsule. I put the crown upside down on the table and gently placed the capsule in the crown. It fit perfectly in the small dent inside. "Strange."

"The capsule fits inside the tooth?" she asked.

I nodded. I left the crown upside down and placed the other half of the tooth into it. "And the tooth fits the crown. With the capsule hidden inside."

"Do you think Vlad knew it was hidden inside?" she asked.

I thought about that before answering. Then I shook my head.

"No," I said. "He didn't ask me about the tooth. And this capsule is probably too valuable for him to forget if he did know about it."

"Why would you say that?" she asked.

"Someone went to a lot of work to hide the capsule," I said. "You don't hide things unless they are valuable."

"That makes sense," she said. "Want to try to open the capsule?"

"I do," I said. I paused, thinking a lot of other things.

"What is it?" she asked.

"It belongs to Vlad," I finally said. "It wouldn't be right to open it. Right?"

"Right," she said.

I didn't tell her what I was really thinking. I was wondering if this hidden capsule had anything at all to do with the fire in the arena. Or with Pookie being hung from the ceiling.

Like some kind of warning.

chapter six

"Ray Hockaday! What brings you here? Looking for a wedding ring?"

I had stopped after leaving the library. Downtown wasn't too far from school.

"Very funny, Mr. Jewel," I said.

Mr. Jewel wasn't his real name, but that's what everyone called him. He owned a small jewelry store downtown on Third Street. The shops were quaint. The sidewalks were brick. There were gas lamps and, in the summer, hanging flower baskets. It was like stepping back in time.

Same thing inside Mr. Jewel's jewelry store. He was in his fifties. He was tall with long flowing gray hair. He had a gray handlebar mustache that he waxed so that it stuck out beneath his nose like horns on a steer. He wore a pinstripe suit, with a vest and bow tie. He looked like a saloon-keeper in a western movie. And he was one of the Tigers' biggest fans. I knew him because I'd bought a couple of watches from him for Christmas presents one year.

"Isn't that something, about the coaching change?" Mr. Jewel said. "What do you think so far?"

His eyes showed his excitement. Mr. Jewel loved to talk hockey.

"Coach Thomas knows his stuff," I said. That was true. Coach Thomas knew exactly what I feared on the ice.

"You like him?" Mr. Jewel asked.

I nodded. Yeah, I liked him. About as much as I liked the thought of putting a needle in my eyeball. But this wasn't something a player said. It always got back to a coach. Besides, if I told Mr. Jewel I didn't like Coach Thomas, then I'd have to explain *why* I didn't like Coach Thomas. And Ray Hockaday, son of the famous "Bear" Hockaday, was not supposed to be afraid of anything.

"So, seriously," Mr. Jewel said. "To what do I owe this pleasure? Anything wrong with the watches you bought?"

"Nothing," I said.

"And no wedding ring?"

"I'm only seventeen," I said.

"Big, strong hockey player like you," he said. "I'll bet there must be a hundred girls hoping you'll ask them for a date."

If only one of them was Amanda. But that was another thought I kept to myself.

"Once I came in here," I said, "and you were repairing a small watch."

"Part of my services," Mr. Jewel said. "But you said you weren't having problems with the watches."

"I remember your workbench in the back," I said. "The big magnifying glass. The tiny tools you used."

"Still there," he said. He grinned. "Thinking of learning a new trade?"

Spying. I kept that thought to myself too.

"Well," I said, "I've got this little capsule."

I pulled the Ziploc bag out of my jean-jacket pocket. The tooth and the crown were in my pants pocket. I didn't want Mr. Jewel to figure out where the capsule came from. That would lead to too many questions.

I put the Ziploc bag on the counter.

Mr. Jewel looked closely at the bag. "You're right. It is small."

"Think you can find a way to open it?" I asked. "And think you can find a way to put it back together so that it won't look like it was ever opened?"

Mr. Jewel stroked his mustache.

"Ray," he said, "if anyone can do it, that would be me."

chapter seven

It was a home game against the Lethbridge Hurricanes. The Tigers were in third place in the standings, easily ahead of the Hurricanes. In terms of playoffs, this wasn't a must-win game. The playoffs were still a couple of months ahead.

In terms of our home crowd, however, it was an absolute must-win. The Lethbridge Hurricanes were our traditional rivals. Tigers' fans loved to see the Hurricanes lose against us just as much as Hurricanes' fans loved it when we lost in their building.

That, however, wasn't the reason I was nervous.

I was at center ice, listening to the singing of the national anthem, and barely able to hear it above the thumping of my heart. We had a new coach and he was going to suspend me if I didn't prove myself to him. Could I play the kind of hockey he wanted? The kind of hockey that my dad wanted?

It didn't take long to find out.

With the anthem finished, I skated to center ice to start the game. The Hurricane center was there waiting for me. He was two inches taller than me, and I knew him well. Joe Tidwell. Long hair. Long reach. A great scorer. And a great fighter.

"How about we drop the gloves?" he asked. "Right now and get it over with?"

I said nothing.

"Sorry," he said. "I forgot. You've never been in a hockey fight."

Again I said nothing. Fear burned in my stomach like indigestion. Why couldn't hockey just be about skating, shooting and passing?

The referee drifted closer.

"Heads up," Tidwell said to me just before the referee reached us. "And I mean that sincerely."

The referee held the puck. Dropped it. As I tried to pull it back with my stick, Tidwell spun around and blocked me, kicking the puck to his left defenseman. I moved to skate past Tidwell, but he shadowed me. He stayed so close that there wasn't any daylight between us. He gave me a jab in the ribs with the butt of his stick.

"See you in the corners," he said. Then, with a burst of speed, he broke for an open spot.

His left defenseman put a pass perfectly on his stick. He took a couple of hard strides, then dumped the puck into the right corner of our end. He put his head down and broke hard across our blue line.

I followed.

The puck took a weird bounce on the boards. Our right defenseman was forced to juggle it briefly. That was enough time for the

Hurricane winger to move into the corner. Both of them fought for the puck.

I hoped the ref would blow the whistle.

He didn't.

That left only one person to go in and help. Me.

Our winger was supposed to stay up near the blue line and prevent a pass back to the point. Our other defenseman would cover the front of the net. That left the center to help out.

It seemed to me that the action was all sticks and skates and bumping bodies. I moved in, looking for a way to chip the puck out along the boards. It would give me some room to skate and look for an open man to feed a pass to.

I stayed on the outside, the way I always did. A part of my mind was telling me to go in with my body. Another part of my mind said that I could get the puck and make a great play.

The hesitation cost me.

The Hurricane winger kicked the puck ahead, squeezing along the boards until he was free. I should have been in closer. Then I could have given him a hip or shoulder check to knock him off the puck. Instead I was too far away to stop him and too close to get back to the slot and help out the other defense.

He made a hard pass. I feebly waved my stick as it zipped past me. I was able to half turn to watch the progress of the puck. It snapped between our other defenseman's legs and onto Tidwell's stick.

He banged it high, over the goalie's shoulder. Just like that, we were down 1-0.

Tidwell raised his arms, wheeling in a tight circle. His eyes met mine. He grinned. He made sure he skated past me.

"Nice try, little girl," he said. "Want to drop the gloves now?"

I knew what he was doing. He was trying to intimidate me. I didn't want to be honest with myself. I didn't want to admit it was working.

The crowd was quiet as our line skated off the ice.

I stepped into the players' box, looking for a place to hide. It didn't do any good.

Coach Thomas paced down the bench behind the players. He put a hand on my shoulder. He squeezed hard, and it felt like an eagle's claw.

"Ray, look at me."

I didn't want to, but I did.

He leaned in close so that the other players couldn't hear.

"Looks like you're not leading the way," he said.

"I thought I had a chance of chipping the puck loose," I said. "We could have moved the puck out and–"

"One thing I hate worse than gutless players," he said, still speaking low, "and that's gutless players who make excuses."

He stared into my eyes. "No excuses, Ray. Got that?"

I blinked. "Got it."

"No ice time either," he said. "Unless you play it my way. Understand?"

He squeezed my shoulder harder and continued. "If you're not in the corners, you're not in the game. Understand?"

Slowly, very slowly, I nodded.

"Yes," I said. "I understand."

He walked away, leaving me to dread my next shift.

chapter eight

For the next two minutes of the game, I hoped for a leg cramp. Vomiting. Another fire to empty the arena. Anything that would delay my turn to go back onto the ice for another shift.

None of that happened.

The Tigers were still down the goal that had been my fault, when the linesman called an offside against the Hurricanes. That meant my line was supposed to go back onto the ice.

I flexed my leg, testing it for the slightest sign of a cramp. Nothing.

I wondered if anyone would notice if I put my finger down my throat to make me throw up. Decided it would be too obvious.

I scanned the rink for smoke. Nope.

All of this meant I didn't have a choice. It was back onto the ice. I skated slowly to our blue line to line up for the face-off against Joe Tidwell. He bumped into me. Not hard enough to get a penalty. But hard enough that I knew it wasn't an accident.

I'd been dealing with this for two seasons. My passing and skating and stickhandling skills were better than most in the league. I knew the word was out that the best way to stop me was to play physical hockey against me. Every game, this kind of stuff happened.

But I still found ways to make plays. I had plenty of assists and goals. I just wasn't a fighter or physical player myself. It hadn't mattered whether I bumped back or dropped my gloves, as long as my line was producing points.

Until Coach Thomas. And this game.

So I bumped Tidwell back.

His head whipped around. He was as surprised as I was.

"What?" he said. "Mama's boy wants some action?"

I kept skating, although I knew he wanted to drop the gloves and fight. I took my position at the face-off. I didn't feel any better about myself for bumping him back, not when it had given him a chance to challenge me like that.

This time, when the linesman dropped the puck, I was able to get my stick on it before Tidwell. I swept the puck back to my left defenseman, winning the draw cleanly.

Tidwell skated beside me and jabbed me in the side with his elbow in revenge.

I ignored it and made a semicircle, then broke for open ice in the center. I took the pass back from my defenseman. With Tidwell coming in hard, I dumped it off to my left winger.

Tidwell bumped me again.

My winger dumped the puck in and I chased it.

I knew what I was supposed to do. Get into the corner and fight their defenseman for the puck.

Normally I'd slow my skating just enough to give the defenseman time to get the puck and move it to the other side. If he didn't have the puck by the time I arrived, there was no point in mixing it up along the boards with him, right?

This time I busted for the corner. Tidwell was right behind me. It put him out of position, but he must have wanted to get me good.

Again, normally this would be a good time to swing back out and cruise for open ice, looking to intercept a pass. But Coach Thomas was watching.

I found a little extra speed.

The glass rattled as I smashed into their defenseman. The crowd roared. The defenseman fell to his knees. The puck squirted loose at my feet. I kicked it to my stick.

Tidwell had committed to coming into the corner, and my right winger was wide open.

The safe play, the one that would protect me, would be to get out of Tidwell's way and let the puck go.

But playing safe was going to get me cut from this team.

I concentrated on the puck. Waited until the last second, then flipped it over Tidwell's stick and along the ice to my right winger.

That left me open, my back to the boards, my chest facing Tidwell.

As he came in, he lifted an elbow. His body slammed into mine, lifting me off the ice. His elbow smashed my head, and my helmet banged against the glass.

I began to fall, and Tidwell hit me with another elbow.

Dimly, I understood that the crowd's noise had risen to another level. On my knees, I saw why. The puck was in the net.

We'd scored.

But that didn't matter. Not compared to the pain that had exploded along my jaw as if I'd swallowed a porcupine filled with dynamite.

I tried to say something. But couldn't.

Warmth filled my mouth. I spat. Saw blood. My tongue hit something sharp.

I spat again. Saw a piece of a tooth.

Seconds later the guys on my team were standing around me. I couldn't get up.

It seemed like forever until the trainer arrived. I kept spitting blood, kept wondering if more pieces of teeth would follow the blood.

When the trainer got there, he helped me to my feet.

"Great play, Ray," he said. "We tied the game, and Tidwell's got a major penalty."

"Great," I mumbled back. My head felt like a busted watermelon. "Really great."

I wasn't there for the rest of the game, but I heard later the Tigers scored two more goals during the power play, and the score stayed 3-1 to the final buzzer.

Somehow that didn't make me feel much better.

chapter nine

The good news was that I hadn't broken my jaw. The bad news was that one of my bottom front teeth had snapped. Dental surgery was scheduled for the next morning, when Dr. Dempster had some staff who could assist him.

In the meantime, Dr. Dempster had given me some powerful painkillers. I wished, though, that the painkillers also worked as sleeping pills.

It was 2:00 AM, and all I could do was stare at the ceiling and try not to think.

Ever done that? The more you tell yourself not to think about something, the more you think about it.

I told myself not to think about Amanda. That made me see her long black hair against the light blue sweater and her beautiful smile. Made me wonder if she would ever go on a date with me instead of helping me with math. Of course, to find out, I'd have to ask her. But I was too afraid she might say no.

Thinking about her made me think about the capsule in the tooth. I didn't want to think about that either, because it seemed it might be a dangerous secret, and danger was not high on my list of things to enjoy. But as soon as I pictured the capsule, I also pictured Mr. Jewel hunched over it at his workbench. And I pictured the tiny sheet of paper he'd pulled from it. There had been some Russian symbols and a string of numbers. Nothing else.

That made me think of Vlad and his reaction to the capsule and the broken tooth.

Mr. Jewel had placed the tiny paper back inside the capsule and screwed it shut again. So I'd given Vlad the tooth and the capsule when I got back to the Moores' house.

Vlad had gone into a Russian shouting fit. Then he'd pulled his fingers across his lips as if he were zipping them shut. He'd pointed at me to make sure I understood he meant I had to keep my mouth shut. He'd said *nyet* about twenty times. Then the scary part. He had slid his finger across his throat as if it were a knife cutting his throat.

Did that mean I would die if I talked about it? Did it mean he would die if he talked about it? Who would do the killing? And why? What did the Russian symbols mean? What could the string of numbers be?

Whatever it was, it meant my guess to Amanda had been right. The capsule was important. Not only important enough to be hidden in a tooth, but, if I understood Vlad right, important enough to kill for.

Or die for.

Nope, didn't like thinking about that.

The tree branches made weird shadows on my bedroom wall. Like in the movie *Monsters, Inc.* That made me think about how, when I was a kid, I was afraid in the dark because I believed in monsters under the bed or in the closet.

Boy, was I wrong about where the monster lived.

The monster was the guy who would come in and spank me until I couldn't breathe because he was mad that his son was chicken. Yeah, my dad. The tough guy.

Didn't want to think about that either. Because then I'd have to think about Coach Thomas. About getting suspended from the team if I didn't play more physical.

Of course, playing physical had just cost me part of a tooth. And the pain from it was the entire reason I was staring at scary shadows on the wall, trying not to think about the pain. Or Amanda. Or the capsule. Or dying. Or getting cut from the team.

It was driving me crazy to be in bed with all those unwanted thoughts rattling through my mind.

Solution?

Get out of bed.

I did. I moved to the window, hoping that looking out at the trees in the moonlight and the river beyond would take my mind off those thoughts.

Instead I saw headlights of an approaching vehicle. About a block away, though, the headlights snapped off. It took a second for my eyes to adjust. Then I saw that it was still moving.

Weird. Why shut the lights off?

It slowed down as it neared the Moore house. Then it stopped. It was a cargo van. White. Like the kind of van that a plumber would use. But this one didn't have any decals on the side. Just plain white. And waiting outside the Moore's house.

Very weird.

It was too dark for me to see who was inside the van. All I could see was a dark outline of a person behind the steering wheel.

Russian symbols and a set of numbers. Hidden inside the tooth of a Russian kid who hadn't known it was there. But who had freaked out once he'd discovered it. Who thought his life was in danger.

Was that a hit man in the van? Watching the house. Getting ready to sneak up with a silcnced pistol?

I shrank back from my window. I was having crazy thoughts. From the painkillers. That was it. Instead of getting loopy, like Vlad, I was going crazy.

Who knew that I knew about the capsule? I ran through a list in my mind. Amanda. Mr. Jewel. Vlad. Surely they hadn't told anyone.

I gulped. There was one other person. A friend, Abe Madison. Computer geek. I'd gone to his house and drawn out the symbols and numbers for him. Asked him to see if he could figure it out. But I had sworn him to secrecy.

Maybe his search for the answer had alerted someone to the secret. That's what happened in movies.

Crazy thoughts, I told myself. Crazy, crazy thoughts.

Still, I grabbed my cell phone. I snuck back to the window to watch the person still waiting in the darkness inside the van. If he stepped out, I'd be calling 911 faster than Pookie had run from the skunk.

Another minute stretched by. My mouth was getting drier each second. My thoughts wilder and crazier.

Then I saw movement. Not from the van, but from the sidewalk.

Someone had stepped from the Moore yard to the van!

I recognized that person almost immediately. It was Vlad. Dressed in sweats. Looking around like he was going to do a drug deal.

Maybe that was it. Maybe it was drugs. After all, I didn't know Vlad that well. No one on the team did. Maybe it was drugs or steroids. That made me feel better than thinking someone had shown up to shoot me.

Then, realizing it made me feel better suddenly made me feel worse. I was so afraid that it made me happy to think badly of Vlad rather than accept that I might be in trouble.

I watched carefully.

The man inside the van reached out. There was nothing that I could see in his hand. Vlad reached toward him. It looked like their hands had touched briefly.

That was it.

They had a brief conversation. Vlad nodded and turned away, back toward the house.

Then the van pulled away. With the lights off.

Like I was going to be able to fall asleep after this.

chapter ten

I had an e-mail waiting for me the next morning. It was from my computer friend. I'd gotten so little sleep, and my mouth was in so much pain, that I found it difficult to see the words on the screen. I read it once. Twice. Three times. I kept blinking to make the letters clear. Even after I was able to focus, it still didn't make sense.

From: Abe Madison <abethebabe@myemail.com>
To: rHockaday@myemail.com
Subject: weird stuff

Ray,

Spent some time in chatrooms with some Russian gamers that I know. Asked them to translate the Russian words you wrote down for me. It said "what did your papa call you when you were a boy." Still don't know what the numbers mean. Maybe some sort of code.

Also, I asked them to look into Vlad's background. He was a star over there, you know. Found out his father died in a mysterious accident. Rumors blamed the Russian mafia for it. What do you think about that?

By the way, now you owe me tickets to the next game.

Abe

I shut down my computer.

Russian mafia?

There was only one person who could give me the answers to this. Vlad. But he didn't speak English. And after last night, it didn't look like I could trust him.

There was a bright side, though.

I was due at the dentist in less than an hour for emergency work on my broken tooth. The pain would at least take my thoughts away from all of this.

"Big hit you took last night," Dr. Dempster said. "Too bad about the jaw."

"Uunnghhh," I answered.

Dr. Dempster had an assistant with him, a middle-aged woman with very nice teeth. She said nothing.

Dr. Dempster, on the other hand, was one of those dentists who liked to talk. I was one of those guys who liked to be polite. Which meant trying to keep up my end of the conversation. That wasn't so easy with a frozen tongue and clamps in my mouth.

"Good thing you had a mouth guard," he said. "This would have been much, much worse. I mean, Tidwell came in at you like a locomotive. But you took the hit."

"Uunngghhh," I said.

"I've never seen you do that before," Dr. Dempster said. "Usually you make plays by being smart, not by being stubborn."

"Uunngghhh."

"This new approach to hockey have anything to do with the new coach?" Dr. Dempster asked, holding a drill just above my eyes. It seemed like a torture instrument, forcing me to answer.

"Uunnngghhh," I said.

"Couldn't tell if that was a yes or no," Dr. Dempster said. "Of course, it's not my business either."

He moved the drill to my mouth. The high-pitched whine drowned out anything else he might have said. I hated this, knowing that the drill bit was grinding away part of my tooth.

I gripped the arm of the chair as hard as I could.

Dr. Dempster kept drilling.

My knuckles began to hurt.

He stepped back. He tapped my knuckles. "White. Very white. Are you feeling any pain?"

I thought about it. The freezing was working. I wasn't feeling any pain.

"Uuunnnggghh," I said.

"Nod your head if you feel pain," he said. "I can give you more freezing. Or shake it if you can't feel anything."

I shook my head.

"What are the chances that you'll just relax?" he said, tapping my knuckles again.

I shook my head.

Although he was wearing a surgical mask that hid most of his face, I could hear the grin as he spoke. "At least you're honest."

More drilling by him. More white-knuckling by me. His assistant suctioned blood and water from my mouth. It seemed to take forever. Finally I just closed my eyes.

About five years later he was finished. He nodded at the assistant, and she left the room.

"The hard part is finished," he said. "We're going to get a temporary cap. That's going to mean first putting a mold in your mouth. She'll be back in a few minutes to do that."

"Uunnngghhh."

"No pain?"

I shook my head again. No pain. Just fear.

"Here's something I learned about pain a long time ago," he said. "You're not going to believe it until you try it sometime. When you try to ignore pain and when you want it to go away, the pain just screams at you. The strange thing is that if you focus on it and try to feel it, it stops being pain. It's just another sensation."

"Uunnngghhh." Like I was going to believe that.

"In other words, welcome the pain. Make it your friend. Once you do that, something else happens. You stop being afraid of pain. And then you stop being afraid."

He pulled off his rubber gloves. He pulled down his surgical mask. He smiled.

"Must be tough," he said, "being the son of a legendary tough guy in the NHL. Everybody expects you to play like him."

I managed a shrug.

"I saw your father play a few times," Dr. Dempster said. "The guy loved to dish it out. He mixed it up with anybody, any time. Of course, he didn't have a choice."

I was very still. Dr. Dempster must have known I was listening closely.

"Yeah," Dr. Dempster said. "He didn't have the skills of most of the other players. He didn't have the skills you do. If he wasn't so tough and mean, he would have never made the NHL."

Dr. Dempster paused. "You, on the other hand, have all the skills your dad was lacking. I'm not sure you should ever try to play his game. I mean, you don't have to be a chicken, but you don't have to be stupid."

He patted me on the shoulder. "But you weren't asking for advice, were you."

I shrugged again.

"As your dentist, however, there is one

last thing I need to tell you. Because I don't want to see you lose any more teeth."

"Uunngghhh." Not much of a response, but it was all I had.

He continued, "I'm sure you've heard it said before. It's better to give than to receive."

I nodded.

"It applies to hockey too," he said. "Think about it."

chapter eleven

Later that morning I sat in a chair across the desk from Coach Thomas. I was wearing a white shirt. I looked like an idiot. There was a big Tim Horton's coffee stain across the front of my shirt. It happened because I had tried to drink coffee when my mouth was still frozen from the dentist appointment. That's not a smart thing to do.

"I don't think I can dress you for our home game tonight," Coach Thomas said, glancing at my stained shirt but obviously deciding not to say anything about it. After all, suspending a player was more important than what the player looked like.

"I don't get it," I said. I pointed at my mouth. "You saw me go into the boards. How much harder can I try?"

"I'm worried about your mouth," Coach Thomas said. "Dr. Dempster's report came in and I'm thinking it would be too easy for another check along the boards to knock the temporary cap off your tooth."

"Dr. Dempster told you that?"

"Your medical records are team information and kept on file," Coach Thomas said. He obviously misunderstood my question. "Our team doctors and team dentists are required to keep us posted on injuries."

"That's not what I meant," I said. I didn't care what Dr. Dempster told him about my medical condition. "It's just that Dr. Dempster didn't say anything to me about that."

Coach Thomas leaned back in his chair. He interlocked his fingers and put his hands behind his head. "By the way, I can tell you not to worry about Pookie."

"Pookie?"

"That's the dog's name, right? The one that was found hanging in the dressing room?"

"Yes, but–"

"Someone dropped off a note at the front office," Coach Thomas said. "It was from a Hurricanes fan who didn't sign the note. The thing with Pookie was supposed to be a joke to rattle the team before you played the Hurricanes last night."

"Thanks," I said. "But–"

Coach Thomas looked at his watch. "Practice is supposed to start in ten minutes. Don't worry. You don't need to skate today either."

He leaned forward again and looked at some papers on his desk. A few seconds later, he looked up at me.

"You're still here?"

"Did Dr. Dempster tell you that I shouldn't play for medical reasons?"

"No," Coach Thomas said. "He just told me about the work he'd done on your mouth.

Asking you to sit out tonight's game was my decision."

"You're worried about my temporary cap falling off?"

"I do care about my players, you know."

"What if I don't care about my temporary cap falling off?" I said.

Coach Thomas leaned back in his chair again. "Are you questioning my decision as a coach?"

"No, but–"

"If you're not questioning me, then I don't see there's anything left to discuss."

He waved me away.

I got as far as the door before turning around. If he had already taken me out of the game tonight, what did I have left to lose by making him mad?

"Yes?" he asked.

"I guess I *am* questioning you about your decision," I said. "I don't think it's fair that you won't let me play. If the cap falls off, too bad. That's my problem."

"So not only are you questioning my decision, but now you're disagreeing with me.

Your coach. Before you answer, you should know I've suspended players for that."

I took a breath. "Yes. I'm disagreeing with you."

He raised an eyebrow. "You want to play that badly?"

"Yes."

"Even after last night. Getting hammered into the boards like that. After spitting out half a tooth?"

"Yes."

"Then I have two things to say," he said, getting up from his chair. "The first is that you shouldn't think you can get away with disagreeing with me like this again."

I nodded. Did that mean I'd just gotten away with it?

"The second is this," he said. "You just passed my test."

"Pardon me?" I said.

"I didn't want you on the ice tonight unless it mattered to you. Obviously it does."

Test, I repeated in my mind. He'd been playing a mind game with me.

"You've got five minutes to get dressed and on the ice for practice," he said. "And don't be late for tonight's game."

chapter twelve

It is better to give than to receive.

That's what I mumbled under my breath halfway through the third period as I squared off against the center for the Portland Winter Hawks in the left face-off circle of their zone. I had been repeating it to myself all game. *It is better to give than to receive.*

Since the opening face-off, I'd been trying to bodycheck players before they body-checked me. I'd discovered that Dr. Dempster was right. It hurt a lot less to hit than it did to get hit.

With the linesman about to drop the puck, however, what I really wanted to give our team was a goal.

We were down 3-2. The Winter Hawks were shorthanded. Most of our hometown fans were on their feet, cheering us on to score during the power play. Somewhere up in the stands, Amanda Kessler was watching too. She'd promised to go out after the game for a milkshake at the Dairy Queen. It would be great to impress her now.

Everyone in the building knew it was important to win the draw and get the puck back to our defenseman. And I knew what this center would try to do to me. His name was Chuck Dianne. He liked to use his size to win the draw. As the referee dropped the puck, he would try to get his stick over mine and then lean down so I couldn't move my stick. Once he had it trapped, he'd swing around with his body and knock me out of the way to allow him to kick the puck into the corner for his defenseman.

One way to beat this kind of center was to be stronger. I wasn't weak, but he had me by at least thirty pounds, and the odds were in his favor. I wasn't going to play into his strength.

My strengths were quick hands and good hand-eye coordination. That's how I'd become a WHL player and how I'd lasted so long in the WHL without playing a physical game.

In this situation, then, I would play my strength against his strength. I'd try to get my stick on the puck before it hit the ice. If it was out of the face-off circle before this center could trap my stick and block my body, it wouldn't matter how strong he was. I just needed to be quicker.

Still, it wasn't that simple. To be quicker, I needed a fraction-of-a-second head start to get to the puck as it was in the air. That required one other skill that set me apart from some of the stronger and tougher players. Observation and memory.

Referees and linesmen all had their own ways of dropping a puck. Some liked to simply open their fingers and let the puck fall. Others liked to give a small throwing motion downward. Still others would lift the puck slightly before slapping it downward. Most centers knew this, and in the seconds before a face-off they watched the hand of the referee or linesman.

Not me.

Long ago, I had decided that, for a referee or linesman, a face-off was more than getting the puck onto the ice. It was also about getting out of the way quickly and without any pain.

Think about it from a referee or linesman's point of view. It's almost like getting ready to drop a steak in front of two lions. As soon as the steak is in the air, there's going to be a lot of movement of sharp and painful things.

If you were going to drop a steak between lions, wouldn't you want to escape as quickly as possible? It's the same with referees and linesmen. Except they're not worried about claws and fangs, but about the flashing blades of hockey sticks, the rising elbows and the scuffling of razor-sharp skate blades as the two centers fight for the puck.

Believe me, I've given this a lot of thought. To move in any direction from a standstill–as a linesman who has just dropped the puck must do–you need to begin by shifting weight. If you're going to move left, you have to get your weight on the right side and push off. Or vice versa. If you want to skate backwards, you need to get the weight on your toes.

That's what I looked for and tried to remember for every linesman and every referee in the WHL. The tiny shift that each of them used to begin to get out of the way. Each one was different, like their fingerprint. It was a secret I kept to myself because I never wanted any of them to figure out what I knew about them.

This linesman was older–in his forties–and he had become a little sloppy with face-offs, and I knew it. In the split second before dropping the puck, his right knee would jerk about a half inch sideways. As if a doctor had tapped him below the knee with a rubber hammer.

The crowd's noise seemed to fade away

as I watched for the little knee jerk. When it came, I did the unexpected.

Everyone in the building knew it was important to pull the puck back to our defenseman. But in the split second it would take for the puck to fall to the ice, it would be nearly impossible to lift my stick high enough to get it in front of the puck and then pull it back.

But not impossible to slap it forward.

The knee jerk came. I reacted to it by lifting my stick blade without even watching for the puck. Instead I was aiming for a spot in the air.

My blade connected with the hard rubber and knocked the puck forward a foot.

Because the Winter Hawk center was trying so hard to get his weight down and trap my stick, he was totally flat-footed. Couldn't move.

I easily sidestepped him.

As the puck hit the ice, I spun sideways, using my hips to block out the Winter Hawk defenseman. That gave me time to get my stick down to the puck. It was on my backhand.

I could have tried a shot, but I was facing away from the net. Toward our defenseman on the point. With the puck on my stick. And an easy wrist shot away from the net toward the blue line.

I flicked it back to the point.

It is better to give than to receive.

I planted an elbow in the Winter Hawk defenseman's belly and fought for position.

Our own defenseman ripped a slap shot. The puck nicked the bottom of the shaft of my stick and changed directions.

The crowd roared.

I'd just deflected the puck into the net. I'd scored!

Three-three!

Their defenseman slammed me in the back with a cross-check. It knocked me to my knees. My stick fell from my hands, and my helmet flipped onto the ice. Their defenseman fell down beside me.

I got up first.

It is better to give than to receive.

If winning the draw and then scoring was smart, what I did next was the opposite.

I decided to get into my first fight in the WHL. Hands still in my hockey gloves, I took a weak swipe at the head of the Winter Hawk defenseman as he was still on his knees.

He roared. Scrambled to his feet. That's when I realized it wasn't the defenseman I'd been pushing in front of the net. It was the other Winter Hawk defenseman. The one four inches taller and forty pounds heavier.

Ooops.

He threw off his helmet. Then gloves.

"Let's go, girlie boy," he said. "I'm ready."

I began to throw my gloves off too. But his first punch was already headed toward my nose.

chapter thirteen

Pain mushroomed through my face as his fist crunched into my nose.

I wobbled and nearly fell down but I managed to keep my balance. I was desperate to shake off my hockey gloves and throw a punch back at him.

He threw another punch as I tried to fling off my gloves. This punch caught me across the eyebrow. Again, it rocked me backward and I barely stayed on my skates.

I tried to throw my gloves off so I'd be able to fight back. But it was like they were Velcroed to my hands.

Another big hammering punch caught my jaw. It caused such a burst of pain that I fell to my knees.

He jumped on my back.

I really wanted to go turtle. To hunch over and put my arms over my face to protect myself. But all game I'd been thinking it was better to give than to receive.

I rolled. And rolled again. Somehow I came up on top of him. I pushed off and got to my feet again.

One last time I tried to throw off my gloves.

Then I realized what the problem was.

I had been so filled with panic that my fingers had immediately formed themselves into fists. It's impossible to throw off gloves when you've already made fists.

I straightened my hands. With quick movements, I flung my arms out again. This time the gloves sailed off.

Now I could take a punch back at him.

Too late.

One last big overhead punch came in with such force it felt like a meteor landing from outer space.

It caught me in the center of the forehead. My feet popped out from under me. I landed on my butt and on my elbows.

Finally the linesmen came in and grabbed the Winter Hawk defenseman. He glared over the linesmen's shoulders at me. I saw blood dripping from his knuckles.

I sat up. Blood trickled down my chin. I felt something loose with my tongue. The temporary cap that Dr. Dempster had put on in the morning.

I slowly got up. I tried to glare back. The linesmen pushed him away.

"Oh, yeah," I said. I spit the piece of tooth on the ice. Felt tough doing it.

"Oh yeah, what?" the defenseman said back to me.

"Don't mess with me again," I said. My lips were split so badly I could barely talk. But I was mad. I was ready to keep fighting. "Or you'll get more of the same."

For some reason, he thought it was funny.

So did the guys on the ice. And the guys on the bench when the guys on the ice told them what I'd said.

But I had the last laugh.

The trainer put ice on my face. After my penalty was over I was able to go back on the ice. I managed to score another goal to win the game.

The Winter Hawk defenseman?

It turned out that a lot of the blood on his knuckles was his own blood. From splitting his skin against my teeth.

And he'd broken a finger with the last punch in the center of my forehead. So he had to leave the game and didn't return.

Yup. Like I told the guys later, it didn't pay to mess with me.

chapter fourteen

In the dressing room at the end of the game, all the aches and pains caught up with me. I guess during the heat of the game you don't notice as much. But when it's over...agony.

I sat on a chair, towel draped over my shoulders. My body felt like it was filled with the glass of broken lightbulbs. My nose was throbbing like I was Rudolph on Christmas

Eve. And the painkillers for my broken tooth weren't doing much except leaving a bad taste in my mouth.

Still, it wasn't going to stop me from meeting Amanda to go for a milkshake. It had taken a lot of nerve to ask her to go to the game and Dairy Queen after, and I was glad she had agreed. I just hoped she'd remember the two goals I scored and not how I'd been a punching bag for the Winter Hawk defenseman. Maybe, if I were lucky, she'd been at the concession during the one-sided fight. But then she would have missed the power-play goal.

I groaned as I stood to get dressed.

"Good game," Coach Thomas said, loud enough for the other guys to hear. "Next time, though, try ducking."

"Hah, hah," I said. Even talking hurt.

The other guys laughed.

Vlad walked up to me. He was already dressed. Jeans. Black T-shirt. Leather team jacket that matched mine. I'd made arrangements for one of the other guys to take him home.

Vlad stopped in front of me. He stuck out his hand, waiting for me to shake it.

I did. I winced because I'd moved too quickly.

"Glad to meet you," Vlad said in a thick accent. "Me, La-Dee-Dah. You, Nail."

"Huh?"

He pointed at himself. "La-Dee-Dah."

He put his finger in my chest. "Nail."

"Yeah, yeah," I said. "I get the whole introduction thing. But my name isn't Nail."

He kept smiling.

"You, La-Dee-Dah," I said, imitating his accent. "Me, Ray-Ray."

Some of the guys were giggling.

"You, Nail," Vlad said. He made some punching motions. "Him, Hammer!"

Now all the guys busted out laughing again. I knew they had coached Vlad on what to say.

I couldn't help it. I started laughing myself. I mean, could I deny it? Next time I'd make a fist after my gloves were off, not before.

"You, Nail," Vlad said again with a broad smile.

"Yup," I said. "Me, Nail."

It was great to be part of a team.

chapter fifteen

"You're lucky not much worse happened," Dr. Dempster said.

I had finally showered and changed. Dr. Dempster was standing over me, using a flashlight and dental mirror to check my bottom teeth. He wore rubber gloves and had wiggled all of my bottom teeth to see that they were still secure.

"In fact," he said, "I should be able to glue that cap back in place until you visit me again on Monday morning for a more complete exam."

He put the dental mirror back into his bag of emergency dental equipment.

He spoke as he looked inside the bag for the special dental glue. "I would, however, still advise you to come to my office right now, where we can make sure everything is fine."

I shook my head.

He grinned. "Amazing how much a girl and a Friday-night date can motivate a person to deal with pain."

I had told him about my date with Amanda. I had asked her to meet me in the parking lot.

I nodded. And it was amazing how much a person was motivated if that person thought he might get cut from the hockey team.

"This won't take long," he said. "And it's just as well. I won't mind going straight home tonight."

He was right. A minute later the cap was back in place.

"You're good to go," he said. "Just don't do anything dumb again tonight."

"Dumb?" I said. The glue tasted a little weird, but it was better than going on a date with Amanda with half a tooth missing.

"Yeah," he said. "Like putting your head in the way of anything else that might hurt you."

If only I had paid more attention to his warning.

"Amanda," I said. "Thanks for waiting."

She was in her car, a green two-door Cavalier. She had rolled her window down. The night air was relatively warm. I was wearing my Medicine Hat Tigers team jacket, and the wind didn't bother me at all.

"What can I say?" she said. "I'm addicted to Dairy Queen milkshakes."

"Oh." So it was the milkshake she was interested in?

She grinned. "Not that I'd go to DQ with just anybody."

"Oh." That made me feel better.

She pointed at her watch. "It's getting late, though. Maybe I should just follow you there. Saves us the trip of coming back here."

"I'd hate for you to sleep in and miss school tomorrow," I said. I was being sarcastic. It was a Friday night.

"It's my mom," she said. "She worries about me."

I nodded. The Tigers didn't have a Saturday-night game, so maybe the guys on the team would be getting together. I'd use my cell phone to try to hook up with them after Dairy Queen.

"Let's go," I said. I was in a good mood. I'd have a chance to hang out with Amanda, then catch up with my friends. I'd survived my first fight, and it looked like Coach Thomas was happy with my new style of aggressive hockey. Things were shaping up nicely.

Until I glanced over the top of Amanda's car and saw a big white van at the corner of the parking lot. Just like the one that had pulled up to the Moores' house the other night.

A large man was walking toward the van. A very large man. I knew that because he had a grip on Vlad's arm. Vlad was tall, but this man was much taller. Much wider.

It didn't look like Vlad really wanted to go to the van.

The large man opened the rear doors of the van. He shoved Vlad inside.

Then he got into the van and began to drive it out of the parking lot.

"Amanda," I said, "have you got your cell phone?"

"In my purse."

"And you've got my cell phone number?"

"Sure," she said. "Why?"

"Call me, please. I don't have time to explain. I can talk to you as we're driving."

"We're not going to Dairy Queen?"

I had begun to unlock my Jeep.

"Not yet," I said. "Vlad might need our help."

chapter sixteen

The white van stopped in a parking lot at Riverside Park, near the Medicine Hat city hall. Here, on a hot summer day, there might be a band playing. There would be moms and dads and kids on the grass, enjoying the nearby river.

On a winter night, however, there was no one. I kept driving and spoke into my cell phone.

"Amanda, keep following me, all right? I'm going to park just down the road."

She and I had been on the cell phone the entire time. I'd explained to her how I'd seen Vlad go out to this van in the middle of the night from the Moores' house. I'd told her that I had no idea what was going on, but that I didn't think it was anything good.

One of the things that bothered me about the van was that it was a rental. From two cars back at one of the stoplights between the arena and the park, I'd noticed the sticker at the back. Was the guy from out of town?

Another thing that bothered me was that paper had been taped on the inside of the rear windows of the cargo van to cover the glass completely. What was in there to hide?

There was only one way to find out.

"Amanda," I said into the cell phone, "would you like to park right behind my Jeep and go for a walk with me?"

We held hands as we walked. I had told her that if the guy in the van saw us coming, it wouldn't look too suspicious. Actually, I liked the excuse to hold her hand.

The stars were bright and, except for the wind, it was nice and quiet. Too bad this wasn't just a walk. Too bad I was so nervous about the situation with Vlad.

We walked closer to the van. The driver wasn't in the front. Neither was Vlad.

"That's weird," I said to Amanda. "We didn't park that far away. I didn't see either of them leave the van."

"Are they in the back?" she asked.

We were close enough to hear some angry words from the cargo van. Words that sounded Russian.

"That answers your question, doesn't it," I said.

"Do we call the police?" she asked.

"Maybe," I said. "But we should know what's happening first. If it's nothing, it will be embarrassing to have the police here. If it's something, maybe the police would get here too late."

"So we look inside," she said.

"Not we," I said. "Me. How about you go back to your car."

"But–"

"I don't know if anything dangerous is happening or not," I said. "You–"

"Don't treat me like I'm a weak girl who needs protection," she said.

"That's not what I meant. If there's danger, it would be smart to have you in a place where you can call the police."

She patted my arm. "Smart thinking."

"I'll call your cell phone from mine," I said. "If neither of us hang up, I'll be able to keep it in my pocket and you can hear everything. If it sounds like I need help, hang up and call the police."

She nodded.

As she walked back to her car, I rang her cell. She answered. I put my cell in my pocket as planned.

Then I snuck toward the van.

I wondered how I was going to see inside without getting noticed. I didn't want to go around to the front of the van and peer through the windshield.

Then I smiled at myself.

Side mirrors. When a person drove, they sat inside and looked backward through the mirrors. So it should work in reverse. I should be able to stand behind the side mirror and look back into the van.

That's what I did. I walked very quietly up beside the cargo van. Because there were no windows on the side, I knew I wouldn't be seen. I crouched beside the van and looked into the side mirror.

It was easier to see inside than I expected. Mainly because there was a light in the back of the van. It looked like a flashlight.

It took a couple of seconds to make sense of everything. But when I figured it out, I didn't like what I was seeing.

The big man was standing in front of Vlad. He had a pair of pliers in his hand. And he was reaching into Vlad's mouth.

chapter seventeen

This was not a situation to call for the police and wait for them to arrive. I knocked on the door. I didn't see any other option. I didn't, however, plan to get into a fight with the monster-sized guy who was holding a pair of pliers. If that happened, I'm sure I would have earned my new nickname of Nail all over again.

I knocked again. There was still no reply from inside.

"Hey, Vlad," I shouted. "Dude! What's happening?"

That would at least let them know inside it wasn't an accident that I was outside the van.

"Vlad! Team party!"

That was the only excuse I could come up with on short notice. Friday night. A Tigers' win. The guys were getting together somewhere. We'd join them.

"Vlad!" I shouted. Knocked on the window.

Finally, movement from inside. I knew this because the van shifted slightly. That gave me a clue as to how big the guy inside was.

He crawled into the front. I heard the locks unclick as he pushed a button inside.

I stepped back from the door as he opened it.

He moved outside. Spoke to me in Russian. He didn't have the pliers in his hand. I knew because it was the first thing I'd looked for—because it was the last thing I wanted to have gripping my nose or my ears.

I smiled and shrugged, hiding my fear. The guy towered over me. The parking lot lights showed a square face, square head, square haircut. Nothing about his face was friendlier than, say, Frankenstein's monster.

"Looking for Vlad," I said. "I saw him get into the van. The guys want him so we can celebrate tonight's win. I tried stopping him in the arena parking lot, but you both got away on me."

The monster man grunted. He put a big, big hand on my shoulder. He pushed me away. I staggered backward. This was a very strong man.

"Hey," I said. "Do you speak English?"

He pointed past me. It was obvious he wanted me to go away. That made it obvious to me that I needed to stay. Back in the van was a pair of pliers. And Vlad. Not a good combination in the hands of this guy.

"Speak English?" I repeated. I needed to pretend I had no clue as to what was happening in the van.

There was another way to find out. "You're ugly," I said. "Like Frankenstein, except worse.

How about I call you Big Frank. Maybe your mother was Big Tank."

He kept pointing but didn't swing at me. He didn't understand the insult.

"Vlad," I said, speaking loudly. "Come on, dude."

I pointed at the van. "Vlad. Us. Celebrate."

I began dancing and singing a song. "Get it? Celebrate."

I realized that Amanda was hearing the entire conversation because of the cell phone in my pocket. She must have thought I was an idiot.

The man grunted one more time. He turned his back on me to get back into the van.

Not good.

The van was unlocked. I'd heard the click.

I took three fast steps and got to the back of the van before the monster could close his door and lock it again.

I popped open the rear doors and swung them wide.

"Vlad!" I said. "Good to see you!"

I reached inside and grabbed his arm.

"Amanda," I said, hoping she was listening to all of this. "Get here. Now!"

I pulled Vlad. The monster inside was climbing from the front toward us. We had to get a jump on this guy before he made it out of the van. I pulled harder and Vlad stumbled onto the pavement.

"Come on," I said. I slammed the rear doors and began running. Vlad stayed with me. We gained some ground on Big Frank.

"See those headlights?" I said to Vlad. "That's Amanda. We'll be safe."

"He will follow me all night long," Vlad said, trotting beside me. "I can never be safe."

We had a big enough jump on Big Frank that he had stopped chasing us. Still, I was too busy running toward Amanda's car to really think about what Vlad had said.

Not until Amanda had dropped us off at my Jeep. Not until Vlad and I were in the Jeep and I had begun to drive away.

chapter eighteen

"Let me get this straight," I said to Vlad as we drove away. "You can understand English."

"I can speak it too."

I tried to remember if I had ever said anything around him that had been mean or embarrassing. Couldn't come up with anything.

Vlad grinned. "Have no worries."

"Huh?"

"You wonder now if there is anything said about me that came from you." He spoke with a heavy accent, of course, and didn't quite put words together like someone who had been born and raised here. But obviously he wasn't lying about being able to speak English.

I frowned at him. "You can read minds too?"

A shrug. "Easy to guess at what you are thinking."

"How about now?" I asked Vlad.

"What is it that you mean?"

"I mean, can you guess at what I'm thinking now?"

"Nyet."

"I'm thinking I should punch you in the mouth. You've been keeping this secret from me since we met. What if I had said something about you that I shouldn't have? Like maybe telling people that I think you're a Russian weenie."

"Weenie? This word I do not know."

"It's a hotdog."

"Ah. Weiner."

"And other people would say weenie means dweeb. Dork."

"Dweeb? Dork?" Those words sounded funny with a Russian accent. "What is dweeb? Dork?"

"Weenie," I said. "Look, that's not fair, letting us talk around you without letting us know you understood every word."

"I do not know who I can trust. Now I do know. You. Always, you protect me with your words. And now you protect me from...what did you call him? Big Frank?"

"I protected you from getting a tooth pulled from your head by a sicko with a pair of pliers."

"Sicko? This word I do not know."

"You know what I don't understand?" I said. "You weren't even trying to fight the guy."

Vlad looked at the floor.

"Come on," I said. "It's not like Big Frank was holding a gun to your head. Or a knife to your throat."

Vlad didn't look up.

"Sure, he was bigger than you," I said. "But it looked almost like you wanted him to pull the tooth."

Then it hit me. Maybe there was more than one capsule hidden in Vlad's mouth.

"You did want him to pull it," I said. Slowly. "You need the other capsule. Or capsules."

It was like I'd taken a stun gun and jabbed it into Vlad's arm. He snapped his head high, stared at me, eyes wide. His long arms began to move in all directions.

"You! You know! Impossible!"

I didn't know much. Except that there had been a capsule in his mouth with a weird message.

"What did your father call you when you were a boy?" I asked.

"I do not understand."

"He had a special name for you."

"Yes," Vlad said. "But what does this matter to what we are discussing?"

I felt my eyebrows crinkle. This wasn't making sense. Unless...

"You don't know what was in the first capsule, do you?" I said.

"Speaking about the capsule can kill you," he said.

"You don't know what was in the first capsule, do you?"

"No," Vlad answered. "I do not want the knowledge. It can kill me. It can kill you. It can kill the players on our team."

"Slow down," I said. "You need to start making sense. Tell me about the capsule."

"First you tell me how you know about it," he said.

I explained how I'd found the capsule, how Mr. Jewel had opened it and how I'd gotten a friend to translate the writing on the paper inside the capsule.

Then he told me his story. And when he was finished, I was afraid.

Very afraid.

chapter nineteen

"Amanda." I was calling her on my cell phone as I drove through the downtown with Vlad.

The reason I was calling was simple.

A set of headlights had been following us for the last ten minutes. I wished it was my imagination. But I knew better. Especially after hearing Vlad's story.

"Ray?" Amanda said. "Is everything all right?"

"I'm sorry our date didn't work out," I said. "I'm glad to hear you made it home."

"Hello? Hello?" This was a female voice.

"Mom," Amanda's voice said on the telephone, "it's all right."

I managed to figure it out. Her mother had picked up the extension. I waited until I heard the click that let me know her mother had hung up again.

"Amanda," I said, "I need help. I can't tell you why. I really need you to trust me."

I glanced in the rearview mirror. Vlad and I were near the public library, passing the beautiful old sandstone buildings around it. The headlights were staying with me. I had a good guess about the driver. Big Frank. The monster with pliers.

"Try me," Amanda said. "Remember, I was there with the white van."

"Your car," I answered. "I need you to park it behind your house. Leave the keys in the ignition."

"You want to borrow my car?"

"There's more," I said. "If you say yes, Vlad and I are going to pull up in front of your house. We're going to knock on your front door."

"You're coming to visit?" she said.

"No," I said. "We're going to take a shortcut through your house. To the back. Then we'll take your car."

"All right," she said hesitantly.

"I can't tell you for how long or where I'm going to take it."

"I didn't ask," she said. "You said to trust you. I am."

"You're beautiful," I said. I coughed. "I mean as a person. To help me."

"Ray..."

"I need to ask something else," I said.

"Go ahead."

"I'm going to call two friends and send them over to your house right now. They're going to park in the back and wait for Vlad and me. After I borrow your car, can you let them take a shortcut through your house and out to my Jeep in front of your house?"

"Yes."

"Maybe let them stay for five or ten minutes."

"Yes."

"You do trust me."

"Yes," she said.

"One of the two guys is going to be tall. Like Vlad. The other guy is going to be shorter, like me. They'll be wearing Tigers jackets because we're going to trade jackets in the back. They'll be wearing our Tigers caps. Could you..."

How could I ask her this?

"Could I what?"

I could ask her because of the headlights behind my Jeep.

"When they leave, could you stand at the front door and give the shorter guy a long hug? Like maybe you were giving me a hug?"

"You're not joking."

"This is important." If she gave the short guy a hug, it would go a long way toward convincing Big Frank that the shorter guy was me.

"I'll do it," she said. She waited a few seconds. "Can I give you some advice?"

"Sure."

"My car has a full tank. Unless you have to get where you've got to go in a hurry, drive out of the city and down a gravel road before you come back to town."

I asked the obvious question.

"Why?" I said into my cell phone.

"Won't be much traffic on a gravel road. If there are no headlights behind you, then you'll know if the switch worked."

I coughed.

"Um, Amanda?" I said.

"Yes, Ray."

"Now I know why I go to you for help with my homework."

"I'd rather it wasn't only because I'm smart."

I grinned into the darkness. "Glad to hear that. Because it's a lot more than that. I think you're beautiful too."

I heard strange noises from the passenger seat. I looked over. Vlad was grinning at me and smooching the back of his hand, making kissing noises.

I hung up the phone.

"Very funny, you Russian moron," I said. "Very, very funny."

chapter twenty

Dr. Dempster stared through the glass of his office door at me. At Vlad. At Mr. Jewel, who was carrying a handbag with some of his watch-repair tools.

Dr. Dempster unlocked the door to let us in. He backed up a step and stared at me with his arms crossed.

"You don't look like you're in pain," he said to me.

"I lied to you," I said. I had called Dr. Dempster at his home from my cell phone. "I'm sorry."

"It's nearly midnight," he said. Arms still crossed. "You woke me up when you called. You *are* aware of both of those things?"

"Yes, sir," I said.

"What's the dental emergency then?" Dr. Dempster looked like he was about to explode. I didn't blame him. I'd told him that one of my other teeth was cracked and that my jaw was swelling, and I had begged for an emergency visit. "Both of these guys seem fine."

"I can explain," Mr. Jewel said.

That startled me. I doubted that even I could really explain all that was happening. And I was the one who had made this plan.

"Please do," Dr. Dempster said, his lips tight. "I fixed Ray's temporary cap right after the game. He assured me then that his mouth and teeth were fine. I certainly don't appreciate leaving my house at this hour. And I can't tell you how angry I am that Ray lied to me over the phone."

"I was worried," I said to Dr. Dempster. "I didn't want you telling anyone at your house the real reason. I didn't want to put anyone else in danger."

"And we are?" he said, obviously not believing it. "Mr. Jewel, who are we in danger from?"

Mr. Jewel looked around. Which was silly. There were only the four of us here, standing in the lobby. I was pretty sure the Russian who had been following us was now at Abe Madison's house, where my friends had taken the Jeep.

"Well?" Dr. Dempster demanded.

Mr. Jewel lowered his voice. "Russian mafia."

"What?"

"Russian mafia," Mr. Jewel repeated.

"That's what I thought you said." Dr. Dempster was still frowning. "What is this, another lie?"

I put up my hand. I felt stupid doing this. It wasn't like we were in school.

"Yes, Ray," Dr. Dempster said.

"If I make a guess about something,

and if my guess is right, will you take us seriously?"

"How can I possibly say yes if I have no idea what you're talking about." He snorted. "Maybe you took a few too many shots in the head in that fight tonight."

"I did," I said. "Way too many. But that has nothing to do with this."

That brought a hint of a smile from Dr. Dempster. "Guess, then."

"When you worked on Vlad's teeth, you took X-rays of his jaw," I said.

"Sure," Dr. Dempster said. "And the sky is blue. Tell me something that's not so obvious."

But Dr. Dempster had lost his frown. In that instant I knew I was right. It came down to the X-rays.

"After you worked on his teeth," I said, "you sent a file over to the Tigers' office with a report on Vlad."

"Again, tell me something that's not obvious." He was testing me now. I knew it. His eyes had widened. Just slightly. Enough to tell me that I finally had his attention.

It hadn't been obvious to me. Not until I'd remembered my talk with Coach Thomas in his office that morning, when Coach Thomas had told me he knew about my dental situation because of the report from Dr. Dempster.

"There was something strange about Vlad's X-ray," I said. "You made a note about it."

"So your guess is right," Dr. Dempster said. "But Russian mafia? That can't be."

"I think," I said, "that someone in the Tigers' organization has been paid to spy on Vlad. Because whatever you put on the dental record you sent to the Tigers' office reached someone in Russia. Who got here a few days later to look for what was shown in the X-ray."

I turned to Vlad. "Tell him."

"This man," Vlad said. "He came to me and told me that everyone on the team would die unless I gave him what he wanted."

"Hang on!" Dr. Dempster said. "Vlad speaks English."

"He speaks English," I said.

I could see Dr. Dempster thinking. I knew what he was thinking.

"Me too," I said. "When I learned he spoke English, I tried to remember if I had said anything in front of him. But there's a good reason he doesn't trust anyone."

"Russian mafia," Mr. Jewel whispered. Like this was an adventure for him.

"Dr. Dempster," Vlad said, "you are a good man. You always said nice things about me."

"Still," Dr. Dempster said, "that's a sneaky thing to do."

"If you were worried about Russian mafia, you would keep secrets too?" Vlad asked.

"Yes," Dr. Dempster said. "I would do the same thing."

Vlad nodded. "This man came to me and asked me for something that I did not have. He did not believe me. He promised to show me how easy he could hurt people around me."

"The fire in the rink," I said to Dr. Dempster. "You heard about it, right? But not the other part."

I told him what had not made the newspaper. The fact that Pookie had been found hanging from the ceiling.

"Yes," Vlad said. "This man from Russia made a good threat. But I did not believe I have what he wanted. He say to me, get codes from capsules. I say back to him, what codes and what capsules. He show me copy of X-ray that brought him here from Russia and ask me where missing tooth was. Then Ray gives me tooth from his pocket. So I call Big Frank to give him one capsule."

The night I'd given Vlad the tooth, Vlad had had that midnight meeting with the stranger outside the Moores' house. Handing him the capsule that I'd found in his tooth.

"Big Frank wanted other capsule," Vlad said. "I tell him if I go to dentist to have other tooth pulled, too many questions for everyone. Don't want people to get hurt because of questions. So I promise to let Big Frank pull it after next game."

I still found this hard to understand. That Vlad had been willing to let Big Frank pull the tooth with a pair of pliers because Vlad was afraid other people might get hurt if they knew about it.

"Then Ray stopped Big Frank," Vlad said. "I ran away with Ray so that Big Frank wouldn't hurt Ray. Now we have to solve problem in different way."

Mr. Jewel was moving from side to side, barely holding his excitement. He looked like a little boy who needed to go to the bathroom. "The capsule," Mr. Jewel said to me. "Tell Dr. Dempster about what was inside the capsule."

"Half of a code," I said, watching Dr. Dempster. "And you saw the X-ray. So you know where the other half of the code is."

Dr. Dempster didn't reply. He stepped to the wall. He hit the light switch and put us in darkness.

"If you're right," he said. "There's no sense advertising to the world all of us are here."

He paused and spoke from the shadows. "Especially if it involves the Russian mafia."

chapter twenty-one

Fifteen minutes after Dr. Dempster first injected freezing into Vlad's lower gum, Vlad nodded. He was ready for the dentist's drill.

Dr. Dempster nodded back and began to work. The sound of the drill seemed very loud this late at night.

It took another fifteen minutes for Dr. Dempster to work the crown loose. He used tweezers to lift it from Vlad's lower jaw. He set the crown on a tray.

"Very good work," Dr. Dempster told Mr. Jewel and me from beneath his surgical mask. "That should have told me to suspect something."

"What do you mean?" Mr. Jewel asked.

"The rest of the dental work in Vlad's mouth is horrible," Dr. Dempster said. "But this crown and the other one were excellent. A lot of money was spent to make sure both crowns would last a long time."

Dr. Dempster used his tweezers to reach into Vlad's mouth again. He pulled out a tiny capsule, identical to the other one that I had found. He did not drop it on the tray, however. He placed it in a small paper cup and handed the cup to Mr. Jewel.

Mr. Jewel winked at us.

"My turn," he said. "With luck, I should be less than five minutes."

Vlad stayed in the dentist chair. He was lying back. His eyes were closed.

"The code in the capsule must be worth a lot," Dr. Dempster said to me. "Someone went to a lot of trouble to hide it. And if someone was sent from Russia as soon as they learned about the capsules from the X-rays..."

"Yes." I didn't add to my answer.

"So you know, then, what Mr. Jewel will find in the capsule?"

"I have a good guess," I said. Mr. Jewel had brought his watch-repair tools with him tonight to open the second capsule as he had opened the first the day before. Although Vlad had explained a lot to me, I decided not to say any more.

Dr. Dempster sighed. "Are you going to tell me about the code?"

"I would rather not," I said.

"Do you have any idea how curious I am?" Dr. Dempster said. "I really, really wanted to ask Vlad about what was inside his crowns when I first saw his X-rays. I made sure he had the tooth to take home so that he would find the capsule. I wanted him to come back and ask me about it."

"But you didn't ask him directly," I said.

"It wasn't my business." Dr. Dempster pulled his surgical mask down. "However, it seems you have made it my business. So I don't mind asking now."

Vlad grunted and shook his head from side to side. Difficult to do anything else in the dentist chair.

"I can translate," I said.

"Let me guess," Dr. Dempster said. "Vlad doesn't want me to know."

"He thinks you would be safer if you didn't know."

Vlad grunted again.

"And," I said, "I think he is also trying to say that the guys on the team will be a lot safer if you don't know."

Dr. Dempster began to pace back and forth. He stopped after a few steps. Maybe realizing what I had just said.

"So you're going to let someone in the Russian mafia take it from him?" Dr. Dempster said.

"Yes," I said. "This is where Vlad is going to need a little more help."

"From me."

"From you," I said.

"Even though you won't tell me what's in the capsule or why I'm doing this."

"The guy came over from Russia and threatened to kill the guys on the team one by one if he didn't get what he wanted," I said. "The fewer people who know about it, the better."

Dr. Dempster thought about it as he stared at me.

He spoke. "Then what do you and Vlad need?"

"For you to hide the capsule by putting it back inside the crown after Mr. Jewel is finished with it," I said. I was doing all the talking because Vlad, of course, could not. "Then put the crown back on so that it doesn't look like it had ever been removed."

"But if the Russian mafia wants the capsule, this guy will have to remove the crown again!"

"Exactly," I said. I thought of the monster-sized guy standing over Vlad with a pair of pliers. "That's why we have one last favor to ask."

"I'm in this far," Dr. Dempster said. "No point turning back now."

"Could you put a lot more freezing in Vlad's jaw?" I asked. "That way he won't feel it when the Russian goon uses pliers on him later tonight."

"You're kidding me, right?"

"No," I said. "If you knew the rest of the story, you'd know I wish I could be kidding."

"Then involve the police," Dr. Dempster said.

Vlad sat up. He shook his head hard and tried talking loudly. I put a hand on his shoulder.

"If you knew all of it," I said, "you'd know that's not an option. If they get the capsule, they'll be happy. But they have to believe Vlad has no idea what was in it. And the only way to fool them is to let them find it where they expect it. Beneath the crown."

"More freezing," Dr. Dempster said.

"Yes," I said. "A lot more freezing. I don't think the guy who wants to yank the crown from Vlad's mouth is much of a dentist."

A killer, I thought, *but definitely not a dentist.*

chapter twenty-two

Although it was well past midnight, all the lights were on at Abe's house. He lived in a nice neighborhood. Lots of big old houses. Cars were parked on both sides of the street. Music seemed to leak from the walls of the house.

As I drove down the street, I saw the white van parked five cars back from my Jeep TJ. The Russian obviously thought that Vlad and I were already in Abe's house. So far, so good.

I wasn't too worried about being seen as we approached Abe's house because I had traded vehicles with Mr. Jewel. We had left him Amanda's car and were driving his old Dodge Caravan. Definitely not a cool vehicle. Definitely not a vehicle you wanted to be seen in by any of your friends. Which made it perfect. Who would think we were in it?

On the passenger side, Vlad ducked down so that, as we passed the white van, it looked like there was only one person in our van. I kept driving and went around the corner. I drove down the alley behind Abe's house.

Vlad and I dashed through the backyard, up the steps and into the kitchen.

Abe's parents were standing at the kitchen counter, slicing cheese and sausages. Louise and William. They were middle-aged. She had bleached blond hair and a deep tan. He wore jeans and a black T-shirt. They worked hard at looking young and cool. In a way, this made them as geeky as Abe. Parents that age should have dressed the way Abe did, and Abe should have dressed the way they did.

"Hey, Ray," William said, giving me a salute that he probably thought was cool too. "Thanks for setting up this party tonight, even if it was on short notice. Abe is pretty happy to be the center of attention for a change."

I nodded. I think what he really meant was that they were happy to be the center of attention. Abe liked the quiet of his computer room. I'd had to beg him to allow people to come over.

Vlad followed me into the living room.

Some of the kids there waved at us. Most didn't. The music was loud. Talking wasn't talking. It was shouting.

Two guys stood in the corner. One tall, like Vlad. One my size. I walked over.

"Thanks, Jimmy!" I yelled. "Thanks, Sam!"

Jimmy and Sam were the two guys who had gone to Amanda's house, going through the alley and backyard to her back door so that the Russian mafia guy couldn't see them. Vlad and I had given them our jackets and hats. Jimmy and Sam had gone out the front and driven my Jeep TJ here so that the Russian mafia guy would follow them. I'd made some other calls to friends on their cell phones to tell them to come here for a party. I'd figured that with enough music and lights in the house, Mr. Russian Mafia wouldn't come inside and try anything.

"You ever going to tell us what this is about?" Sam yelled back. He was the tall one, Vlad's height.

"No!" I yelled. "I'll just owe you both a favor, all right?"

They nodded.

"Hey," I said. "We need our jackets and hats back."

Too soon, Vlad and I would be going outside again. To the Jeep. Knowing that the Russian mafia monster would follow us to a place where he thought we wouldn't be safe.

chapter twenty-three

As I'd predicted, Abe was in his computer room. He was wearing headphones. His back was toward us. He was facing his computer screen.

I walked into the room. Vlad was behind me. I locked the door. Abe didn't move.

I tapped Abe on the shoulder.

He jumped halfway out of his chair. He landed. He took off his headphones.

"What were you listening to?" I asked.

"Silence," Abe said. He gave his head a shake. "Too much noise in the house. I mean, do people actually enjoy parties?"

"Your parents," I said.

He snorted. "Yeah."

I pointed at the screen. "Do you think you have it set up?"

"I'm afraid to say it," he said, "but yes. I'm using an IP address that I'm running through a server that I've hacked into that belongs to a college in England. Through there, I've found a way behind a firewall of a newspaper computer in Alabama, using a Trojan horse that is impossible to detect. From that computer, I'm relaying through a mainframe in Argentina and–"

"Abe," I said, "I just need to know there's no way in the world to track us to this computer in this house."

"Um, basically."

"Basically?" I said. "We need a hundred percent guarantee here. Basically isn't good enough."

"How's this?" he answered. "If we stay online for less than ten minutes, there's not a security expert in the world who could follow the trail back here."

"That's what I wanted to hear," I said. "Then we're ready."

"To go where?"

"Kuwait," I answered.

"Kuwait," he repeated.

"More specifically, a bank in Kuwait," I said. "Trust me."

Abe glanced at Vlad, then back at me. "How do you know?"

Abe didn't know that Vlad knew English. It was a secret I'd keep for Vlad.

"I'm sure," I said. At least, I was sure according to what Vlad had already explained to me. "Trust me."

"A bank?" Abe said.

"A bank."

"Online?" Abe asked.

"Unless you would prefer to walk."

"Online it is," Abe said. "Got an internet address?"

I gave it to Abe. His fingers flew over the keyboard. The computer screen brightened, then dimmed, then brightened.

Abe read out loud, "Commercial Bank of Kuwait. Cash link service. Fixed deposit interest rate inquiry. Limit inquiry. Balance inquiry. Funds transfer. This the stuff you're looking for?"

I glanced at Vlad. He gave me a nod too slight for Abe to notice.

"That's it," I said. "How about balance inquiry."

"To find out how much money is in the account?"

"Yes."

Abe tapped the keyboard again. "It needs a user name and password."

I took a piece of folded paper from my back pocket. I unfolded it. I put it on Abe's desk.

"Vladinsky," Abe said. "This is the user name?"

"Try it," I said. "And there's the ten-digit password."

I put a hand on Abe's shoulder. "Go slow. Don't make a mistake."

"I don't make mistakes," he said. "Not at any speed. That comes with being a geek."

I leaned over his shoulder and watched the computer screen. Seconds later, a number appeared on the computer screen. A very big number.

Abe spun his chair around and faced us.

"Ray," he said, "that's over twelve million dollars."

I wasn't good at math. But I was good enough to know that all those zeroes meant he was right.

"It's in a bank in Kuwait," I said.

"You don't understand," Abe said. "We are in this account. Remember earlier when I said 'funds transfer'?"

"I remember," I said.

"That means you can send this money anywhere. Right now."

"Anywhere," I repeated.

"Sure," Abe said. He was trying to act casual. But I could see he was scared. "By entering the right user name and password, it's as if the money is yours. If you've got another account somewhere that can take the transfer, all I need to do is give this online account instructions where to send it."

I closed my eyes and rubbed my face. Twelve million dollars.

"Ray," Abe said. "People will kill for money like this."

chapter twenty-four

"Ray," Abe said. "Ray, what is going on here?"

I was standing at his window, looking through the blinds and down the street at a parked white van.

"Abe," I said, stepping away from the window. "Give me a second or two. I need to think."

Abe was right about one thing. People would kill for a twelve-million-dollar bank account. In fact, after hearing Vlad's story earlier in the night, I knew that at least one person had already been killed for it. Vlad's father. Now it looked like Vlad might be next. Or guys on the hockey team.

Still, it didn't seem right to let the Russian mafia just take the money.

"Ray," Abe said.

I put up my hand to keep Abe from talking. An idea was coming to me. Mr. Russian Mafia couldn't take the money. Not right away. He needed the user name and password. Then he'd have to find a way to get that information to the people back in Russia who had sent him here. If there was some way to delay him, and if the delay was long enough...

"Abe," I said, "how long would it take for you to set up a new account at another online bank where we could transfer money from this account?"

"Are you thinking of stealing the money?" There was awe in Abe's voice. I guess twelve million dollars will do that to a person.

"No," I said. "That would be very, very stupid."

"Not that stupid," he said. "It's a lot of money."

I looked at Vlad. "Can I tell Abe how the money got there?"

Vlad nodded.

Abe frowned. "Vlad understands English?"

"When you find out how that money got into the account, and why Vlad had the user name and password hidden in his teeth, you'll understand why he keeps everything in his life so secret."

"Hidden in his teeth!"

"In his teeth," I said. "Are you going to listen? Or make me keep repeating things?"

"Listen," Abe said.

So I told Abe everything that I'd learned from Vlad.

He'd grown up in a shipping town called Taganrog, a port on the Black Sea. It had become a hotbed of criminal activity after the collapse of the Soviet Union. His father had been part of the Russian mafia there.

When Vlad was ten, his father had taken him to Moscow to get some dental work done. Shortly after, Vlad's father had died in a car accident that probably wasn't a car accident. When some Russian mafia showed up to ask Vlad about missing money and the password and user name for a bank account, Vlad had told the truth. He didn't know anything about it. It probably helped that he was only ten, and they couldn't be sure if his father had passed on any secrets. Still, Vlad knew enough about the Russian mafia to know if it involved money stolen from them, they would always be watching him.

When I was finished, Abe's eyes were wide. "They've been waiting six years."

"Not waiting," I said. "Watching. Spying. Just on the chance that Vlad had the information and would someday try to draw the money from the account. I'm guessing they paid someone here to keep spying on him, and that someone must have reported back to Russia about strange capsules in the X-rays. Three days later, a guy in a white rental van shows up. Tells Vlad to give up the information or guys on the hockey team start dying. That's when Vlad realized he had the missing information in his teeth."

"Not a good idea to steal money from them," Abe said.

"No. Every day for the rest of your life you would be wondering when they would show up to take it back. And you'd be wondering exactly what they might do to you. Which is why Vlad was so willing to give Big Frank the capsules. Vlad knows he's got a great shot at pro hockey."

Abe shivered. "Make your money in pro hockey and you don't have to worry about Russian mafia taking revenge for stolen money."

I thought of poor Pookie, hanging from a skate lace in the dressing room. I thought of how the guy in the white van had threatened Vlad that he would do worse to the players on the team.

I smiled at the thought of making this guy pay for it.

"Wouldn't it be great," I said, "if it looked like someone else had stolen the money?"

chapter twenty-five

Vlad and I left through the front door of Abe's house. We were wearing our Medicine Hat Tigers hockey jackets and Medicine Hat Tigers hockey caps again.

I had the car keys in my pocket. We walked directly to the Jeep. We got in and drove past the man in the white van. Seconds later the headlights of the van came on. The van pulled out and followed us.

I drove toward the Trans-Canada Highway. Vlad still wasn't saying much. Maybe he didn't like my plan. Maybe his mouth was so frozen from the dentist that he couldn't talk. Maybe he was afraid. I didn't ask.

The headlights of the van stayed close behind. The driver obviously didn't care that we might know we were being followed. And why should he care? He knew that Vlad couldn't run from him forever.

But for our plan to work, there were a lot of things I hoped the driver didn't know. Like that we had not been at the party, but at the dentist. And that we had figured out exactly what had been hidden in the crowns of Vlad's teeth.

I had to keep driving as if I didn't know about the driver or his intentions. So on the Trans-Canada, I headed south. Our destination was the Saamis Teepee.

This was the world's largest teepee. It was built of steel and was twenty stories tall. It was named for the *Saamis*, a Blackfoot Indian word for the headdress of eagle tail feathers worn by a medicine man–the medicine hat. It was painted white for purity, red for the rising and setting sun, and blue for flowing waters. It had been built for the 1988 Olympics in Calgary, Alberta, then moved to the city of Medicine Hat. It could withstand winds of 150 miles per hour.

Vlad didn't appear interested in those facts as I explained them to him. I realized I was talking for the sake of talking because I was afraid. So I shut my mouth and drove.

Our plan was simple. When we got to the parking lot, Vlad was going to leave the Jeep and walk up toward the teepee. This would force the Russian mafia guy to follow him. That would leave the white rental van empty.

My job was to run to the van and find the rental papers. All we needed was the guy's name. Then I would call Abe with my cell phone and give him the spelling of the Russian's name. We were going to open a bank account for him. Maybe we would have been smarter just leaving all of this alone. But there were no guarantees that giving Big Frank the information would end all of this for Vlad. It would be much better to find a way to give Vlad some insurance. Like moving the money somewhere else.

If Big Frank locked the van before chasing Vlad, I would use a rock to bust the window and break in. Yes, that was wrong. But compared to the threat this guy was to Vlad and our hockey team, it seemed necessary. I wasn't too worried that he would report the damage to the police.

Vlad had the tough job. He had to let himself get caught and then allow Big Frank to use those pliers to pull his crown out of his mouth. Freezing or not, I didn't know if I could do that. Just thinking about a guy pinning me to the ground and jamming a pair of pliers into my mouth was giving me the shivers.

It was a pretty good plan, I thought.

Except for one thing.

When we parked and Vlad got out of the Jeep and began running toward the teepee, Big Frank didn't chase him.

Instead, Big Frank walked up to the Jeep with a tire iron in his hand.

I locked my door. Then leaned over and locked Vlad's door. I wanted to drive away, but I couldn't. That would mean leaving Vlad all alone with the monster.

Big Frank tapped on my driver's side window with the tire iron. It was a gentle tap, but it sounded like thunder.

I shook my head.

He lifted his hand. Swung the tire iron down. I barely managed to shift out of the way as it crashed through the window. Pieces of glass sprayed my leather hockey coat and my head.

He reached in to unlock the door. What made it more frightening was his total silence.

I tried to scramble over the gearshift to the other side of the Jeep, but I still had my seatbelt on.

Big Frank popped open the door.

I felt the breeze of the cool night air. Saw the brightness of the stars over his shoulders. It was so peaceful at the teepee. But not at my Jeep.

I fumbled with my seatbelt. It clicked open. Maybe I should have left it on. He dragged me out of the Jeep. He pushed me up against the side. He yelled something in Russian over my shoulder. Like he was telling Vlad he had me.

I took a swing at him.

That was as dumb as undoing my seatbelt.

He grunted as my fist hit his ear. But that was it. Only grunted. Didn't fall down. Didn't let go. He was big.

He lifted the tire iron again. This time it wasn't to smash my window but my head.

I tried ducking but the tire iron caught me on the side of my face. The pain was beyond description. I couldn't even scream. I fell to my knees. Then onto my elbows.

Big Frank kicked me in the ribs. Twice. Maybe more. But after two kicks I didn't feel anything except for blackness closing in on me.

chapter twenty-six

I regained consciousness just before the van started moving. I was in the front seat on the passenger side, slumped against the seatbelt. The Russian must have buckled me in to keep me from falling over.

My jaw was broken on the left side of my head where the Russian mafia guy had hit me. I'd never had a broken jaw before, so I shouldn't have known that it was broken.

Except there was no other explanation for the pain tearing through the side of my head.

My left eye was swollen shut too. To see, I had to turn my head to look out of my right eye. Moving my head made me so dizzy I nearly threw up.

Vlad was behind me. I only knew this because I recognized his shoe, sticking up in the middle of the floor of the backseat.

"Vlad, you okay?" I said. Talking sent spears of pain through my head. My words seemed to come out as a mumble.

"He got my tooth," he answered. "Otherwise, I am alive."

Big Frank shouted at me in Russian. Then shouted at Vlad.

"He says if you talk anymore," Vlad told me, "that he will hit you across the head again. He says if I try anything from back here, he will kill you with the knife in his pocket."

The van was moving out of the parking lot now. Back toward the highway. I wanted to close my eyes in the darkness. I wanted to be unconscious again, where it didn't hurt like this.

But I needed to think. Something was wrong about this besides the very, very obvious.

Big Frank had what he needed from Vlad. But he'd gone to the effort of putting Vlad and me in the van. He could have just as easily left us behind at the Saamis Teepee. When I realized that, I realized what it meant. He wasn't taking us somewhere to give us a reward for being nice boys. He was taking us somewhere to make sure we'd never be able to tell anybody about what had happened. Ever. Probably going to make sure no one would ever find our bodies. I'd been right. Giving Big Frank the information hadn't been enough to make it safe for Vlad. Or now for me.

I didn't see a choice. I had to speak to Vlad. I braced myself for the pain of speaking with a broken jaw. And for the pain of getting hit across the head by Big Frank.

I spoke as loudly as I could. "Vlad, move your left foot if you think he's going to kill us."

Big Frank backhanded me with as much force as a regular person's full punch. It knocked my head against the seat. Then I slumped forward with only the seatbelt holding me in place. Tears ran down my face at the pain. I could hardly breathe.

I turned my head enough to see Vlad's left foot between the seats. He was moving it back and forth. Big Frank was going to kill us. Once he got the van back on the highway, it would only be minutes until we were away from the lights of the city. There were hundreds of square miles for him to take us and hide our bodies.

Think, I told myself. *Think!*

But the pain was so bad I couldn't concentrate.

Dr. Dempster's words came back to me. *When you try to ignore pain and when you want it to go away, the pain just screams at you. The strange thing is that if you focus on it and try to feel it, it stops being pain. It's just another sensation.*

Pain. I was so afraid of it. My head and jaw hurt so badly that I wanted to break down and sob like a baby. And I was afraid of how much it would hurt when the Russian mafia guy stopped the van and forced us to walk somewhere before killing us.

Dr. Dempster's calm voice seemed to speak to me. *In other words, welcome the pain. Make it your friend. Once you do that, something else happens. You stop being afraid of pain. And then you stop being afraid.*

So I started thinking about the pain. I tried to feel it. I tried to be curious about it, and, strangely enough, the pain started to fade. It's not like the sensations disappeared. No, I was still aware that there was something very wrong with my jaw. But the pain stopped overwhelming me.

I was able to think.

I lifted my head. Up ahead were the tall streetlights at the exit ramp that led to the highway. There wasn't much time. What could I do?

I couldn't stay sitting up. I slumped forward again. The seatbelt cut into the skin of my neck.

Seatbelt!

We did have a chance. A very slim chance. But that was better than no chance.

I'd have to warn Vlad, though. I knew that Big Frank would hit me again. That the pain would tear me apart like a hand grenade going off in my skull. But I couldn't allow myself to let the fear of that pain stop me.

I straightened to get a look at the road ahead. I waited until Big Frank began to slow down to turn onto the exit ramp. I drew another breath to speak to Vlad. Spoke with all the energy I had left inside me.

"Vlad, make sure your seatbelt is on. And yell at him to distract him."

Big Frank yelled at me again and swiped my head with another backhand. Once again it snapped my head back.

I groaned and fell forward. I hoped Big Frank thought that meant I had passed out again.

Vlad began shouting at Big Frank in Russian.

Head hunched down, I reached across for Big Frank's seatbelt lock. My thumb hit it and it unclicked. He didn't seem to notice. Somehow I found enough strength to raise myself up again and look through the windshield.

There was a light post to our right.

Vlad was yelling at Big Frank, and Big Frank was yelling at him. This was the only chance.

I screamed. Turned. Grabbed the steering wheel. Yanked the top of it toward me with both hands. Held on as Big Frank fought to keep control of the van.

The tires screeched as the van swerved, and he desperately tried to hit the brakes. Still, I held on. I let my full body weight drag the steering wheel to the right.

The van left the road. Whizzed through the air.

I looked up. The light post filled my vision.

BANG!

The van hit the concrete base of the light post and came to an instant stop.

For a split second I thought I had gone through the windshield. But the giant fist that hammered my chest was the air bag. It popped me back against the seat and deflated.

Then silence.

There was a groan beside me. The driver's side air bag had saved Big Frank from going through his windshield. But without a seatbelt he'd been thrown against the driver's door. Blood was running down his face.

He opened the door and fell to the ground.

Safe, I told myself. Safe.

A second later he was leaning back into the van. He had a knife. Big Frank lifted it upward to stab at me.

Then the sound of a car horn.

He stepped back into the glare of headlights.

"Hey, buddy!" came a voice. "You all right?"

Footsteps. The person who had stopped the car came running toward our wrecked van.

"Hey!" said the same voice. "What's with the knife?"

Suddenly someone was thrown into the van beside me.

Big Frank left on the run. Seconds later I heard a car door slam. Then screeching tires again as he gunned it.

The guy thrown into the van found his balance. He jumped out of the van and started running after his car.

"Hey!" he shouted. "Are you crazy? Come back here."

"Vlad," I said. The edges of blackness were closing around my vision. "Are you all right?"

"I'm alive," he said.

"Find the rental papers before the cops get here." It seemed like someone else was speaking. Even my pain was going away as I began to fade. "Get the guy's name. Call Abe with my cell phone. Make sure Abe knows his name."

That took too much out of me.

I closed my eyes and didn't fight it anymore. It felt like I was getting swept away by a river. A dark deep river.

It pulled me under and I was gone again.

chapter twenty-seven

Two weeks later the Hurricanes were back in the Hat. I'd missed all the games since the night of the crash of the van. It wasn't that I'd been hurt because of the accident; I hadn't been and neither had Vlad. Although the tire iron against my head had not broken my jaw, I had needed a lot of dental surgery to fix things up. It had taken all this time for me to finally be cleared to play.

There'd been plenty of questions following that night, but Vlad and I had said nothing to the media and very little to the police. Only that some Russian guy we didn't know had gone psycho on us. This was true, of course. We just left out the reasons why. Dr. Dempster and Mr. Jewel had said nothing. Amanda and Abe had done a good job of keeping the events of that night secret too. The attention had finally gone away, and it looked like there wouldn't be any more questions.

Now I was on the ice for a game again. It was great to be in a mental zone where all I had to worry about was hockey.

And to worry about Joe Tidwell. The Hurricane center faced me as the referee was getting ready to drop the puck to start the game.

"Hey, little pussycat," Tidwell said. "Ready to get mashed again?"

I ignored him. My focus was on the referee's right skate. This guy was a skate wiggler before dropping the puck. I wanted to sweep the puck clean to my defenseman.

"Cat got the chicken's tongue?" Tidwell said to me.

"Enough," barked the ref.

"He needs you to protect him?" Tidwell asked the ref. "Little chicken like him?"

"Want an unsportsmanlike conduct penalty?" the ref asked in return.

Tidwell was smart enough to clamp his mouth shut. He settled in to try to win the draw against me. The crowd was chanting. I let the atmosphere of the game and the nervousness of needing to play well settle on me. Before, this would have filled me with fear. Now it made my concentration sharper.

The ref's right skate gave a telltale wiggle. I made my move as the puck fell. I picked it clean out of the air, spinning it back to my defenseman. I turned my hip, making sure to block Tidwell's move past center.

He shoved my back with a vicious cross-check. I stayed in front of him until our defenseman had time to clear the puck. Then I headed up-ice to an open position. Tidwell shadowed me.

The puck went to our left winger. I broke fast. He hit my stick with the puck at the blue line.

I saw an opening between the two Hurricane defenseman. I had full speed and wanted to use it.

I dropped my shoulder as if I was going outside. The safe way. The way I would have always gone before.

But I pushed the puck ahead between them and found one extra gear to go up the dangerous middle. As I squeezed past the defensemen, one of them gave me a stick in the ribs.

Now I was in on the goalie.

Quick fake to my backhand. Puck to the forehand side. Hard wrist shot that caught the upper corner.

Goal! Off the opening face-off!

I lifted my hands to celebrate and began a swooping turn back to the bench.

Tidwell banged me hard, throwing me into the boards. I crashed to my knees.

Before, I would have looked for a place to hide. Not now. The worst had been dealt to me that night in the cargo van, and I'd discovered the fear was nothing I couldn't survive.

Tidwell stood over me. "Come on," he said. "Let's go."

Icy rage filled me instead of fear.

I got to my feet. I dropped my gloves. I slowly took off my helmet. Yeah, it would hurt if my teeth got busted up again. But I could deal with that now.

I moved in on Tidwell. He was so surprised, he backed away. Only the net stopped him.

The linesmen gave us room. The crowd was roaring.

I moved real close to Tidwell.

"You get the first punch," I told him. I left my hands at my side. This was a new feeling. Of control. Of being ready to take any pain. Of anger at all the times I'd been pushed around by hockey players who wanted to intimidate me. "Better make it a good one. Because that's all you're going to get."

Tidwell had a shocked look on his face. My reaction must have surprised him, because his punch was slow. Or maybe I was in a zone of concentrated anger and was reading Tidwell's body language the way I read referees before they dropped the puck.

His left shoulder dropped, and that gave me plenty of warning. I ducked the punch and bulldozed into Tidwell. His skates hit the bottom of the net and he fell hard on the ice.

Just like that, I was sitting on his chest. His legs were pinned beneath my knees. I had an open shot to begin raining punches into his face.

"Tidwell," I said, "you're a loser."

Instead of punching him, I patted his cheek lightly with my right hand and smiled.

"Next time," I said, "mess with someone else."

Then I stood and let the referee take me to the penalty box.

chapter twenty-eight

Dr. Dempster met me after the hockey game. He'd waited until I was alone to catch up to me in the hallway.

"Dr. Dempster," I said. "How are you?"

"I've been enjoying your new brand of hockey. Tough, but smart."

I grinned as well as I could, considering the work that he'd done on my jaw. "It's better to give than to receive."

"As long as you keep your teeth," he said. "I'd hate to see all my good work wasted."

"Nothing hurts," I said. "If that's what you're asking."

"Nope." He had a mysterious smile. "That's not why I came looking for you."

I lost my smile.

"No worries," he said. "I've kept the secret."

Still, I didn't like this.

"But I haven't lost my curiosity," Dr. Dempster said. "I keep wondering what was so important that the guy would come here all the way from Russia and do what he did."

I shrugged.

"What I find more curious is that he hasn't been back."

"His name was all over the papers," I said. The police had tracked him from the rental car, then backward to the airline flight. "He knows he shouldn't show up here again."

"No one else has shown up either," Dr. Dempster said. "Aren't you worried about that? I mean, the Russian mafia doesn't strike me as an organization that would quit just because it failed once. You'd think they'd send someone else."

"Not worried," I said.

"I think I know why," Dr. Dempster said. "You don't have to tell me if I'm right, but at least humor me. You owe me that."

"More than that," I said.

"I have friends on the police force," Dr. Dempster said. "They've let me in on a small piece of information that has been given to them by the Russian police. It probably won't make the papers, so don't tell anyone else."

"Sure," I said. I'd been very good about keeping the rest of it secret.

"It seems," Dr. Dempster said, "that this man–Alekseev Borodin was his name, right?–has turned his back on a life of crime."

"Really," I said. "Maybe my face hurt his tire iron so badly it scared him away from attacking other people ever again."

Dr. Dempster smiled. "Must have been it. It looks like he's not only quit hurting people, but he's begun helping people."

"Really. What a nice story. Got to go. I have a date with Amanda."

"Hang on," Dr. Dempster said.

I waited.

"What the Russian police reported was that Alekseev Borodin made a very public donation of twelve million dollars to an organization that oversees orphanages all over Russia."

"Look at the time," I said.

Dr. Dempster's smile grew wider. He knew he had me.

"Do you think that's a coincidence?" Dr. Dempster asked. "If I remember right, wasn't Vlad raised in an orphanage in Russia?"

"Could be." I was squirming.

"Just thought you should know," Dr. Dempster said. "Oh, and one other thing. Although the money came in as a donation from the bank account of this Alekseev Borodin, he's never come forward to accept thanks from the organization."

"Imagine that," I said. "It's almost like Alekseev Borodin somehow stole twelve million dollars from the Russian mafia, then gave it away, and now they're looking for him instead of Vlad."

"Yeah," Dr. Dempster said. "Imagine that."

More titles in the Orca Sports series

All-Star Pride
by Sigmund Brouwer

Jumper
by Michele Martin Bossley

Rebel Glory
by Sigmund Brouwer

photo: Bill Bilsley

Sigmund Brouwer is the prolific, best-selling author of books in a number of genres. He lives in Red Deer, Alberta, and Nashville, Tennessee.

Sigmund enjoys visiting schools to talk about his books. Interested teachers can find out more by e-mailing: authorbookings@coolreading.com